THE ULTIMATE
LOS ANGELES DODGERS
TRIVIA BOOK

A Collection of Amazing Trivia Quizzes
and Fun Facts for Die-Hard Dodgers Fans!

Ray Walker

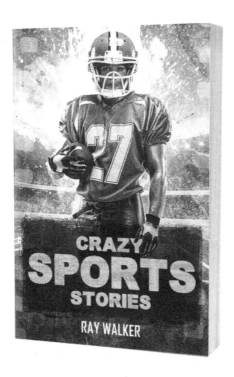

CONTENTS

INTRODUCTION

Obviously, you're inspired by your favorite team. In this case, the team in lights is none other than the Los Angeles Dodgers, one of the original franchises in the National League, and surely one of the best ever in the entire glorious history of Major League Baseball (although archrival San Francisco Giant fans might want to argue just a bit about that claim).

Los Angeles, "the City of Angels," has always been filled with winning pro teams: the inimitable Los Angeles Lakers and their 16 NBA championships, more recently the Clippers (enticed from San Diego), the Kings flying around the Staples Center ice, the MLS Galaxy, the L.A. Rams (wooed back from St. Louis), and, of course, the Los Angeles Angels just down the freeway in Anaheim

But the Los Angeles Dodgers are extra special. There's no place in the world to play hardball like their massive home park, Dodgers Stadium in Chavez Ravine, filled with screaming Los Angelinos. And, since the Dodgers arrived out west, they seem to have just become better and better. The heart-breaking World Series upsets in 2017 and 2018 were tough on Dodgers lovers, but after seven straight seasons atop the NL West, 2019 saw the Boys in Blue bashing all kinds of records, including most runs scored in the NL and fewest runs allowed in all of MLB.

Next year, the L.A. Dodgers will celebrate 138 years of existence at (or near!) the peak of the baseball world and you'll be there, armed with all the trivia and fun facts on their colorful players, big signings and trades, and the incredible emotional highs and lows of a world championship team. The Dodgers have had more than their fair share, like the "Battle of Chavez Ravine." And there are many more merry moments (like the latest World Series win in 1988 and near misses in 2017 and 2018) to quiz your friends and family about.

Clearly, you may use the book as you wish. Each chapter contains 20 quiz questions that are a mix of multiple-choice and true or false formats, an answer key (don't worry, it's on a separate page!), and a section of ten "Did You Know?" factoids about the team.

For the record, the information and stats in this book are current up to the beginning of 2020. The Dodgers will surely break more records and win many more awards as the seasons march on, so keep this in mind when you're watching the next game with your friends. You never quite know: Someone could suddenly start a conversation with the phrase "Did you know…?" And you'll be ready.

CHAPTER 1:

ORIGINS & HISTORY

QUIZ TIME!

1. In what year were the Dodgers established?

   a. 1875

   b. 1883

   c. 1901

   d. 1911

2. The Dodgers have won numerous NL pennants and World Series in their illustrious history. How many World Series championships have they won, to be exact?

   a. 4

   b. 6

   c. 9

   d. 12

3. The Dodgers and General Manager Branch Rickey made history by signing Jackie Robinson, smashing MLB's long-standing "color barrier." In what year did they sign the first African-American player ever?

a. 1945

b. 1947

c. 1953

d. 1957

4. When the Dodgers still played in Brooklyn, with what other club did they develop a natural rivalry?

a. The New York Cosmos

b. The New York Yardbirds

c. The New York Highlanders

d. The New York Giants

5. Which ballpark provided an intimate home for the club from 1913 to 1957?

a. Brooklyn Field

b. Ebbets Field

c. Ebenezer Field

d. Yonkers Yard

6. While still on the East Coast, how many times between 1949 and 1957 did they finish first or second in the NL in home attendance?

a. 3

b. 5

c. 7

d. 8

7. Despite the team's persistent popularity in the East, what was the primary reason that Dodgers owner Walter O'Malley decided to make the big move to the West Coast?

a. He wanted to escape the stiff Eastern competition.

b. He wanted to take advantage of the low tax burden in CA.

c. He wanted to take advantage of the fan base left after the Gold Rush.

d. He wanted to take advantage of MLB's lucrative expansion to the West Coast.

8. In what year did the Dodgers finally break through to overcome the dreaded Yankees and win their first-ever World Series?

   a. 1935

   b. 1945

   c. 1950

   d. 1955

9. Where did the Dodgers first play baseball in Los Angeles before moving to their present home called Dodgers Stadium?

   a. The L.A. Memorial Coliseum

   b. The Rose Bowl

   c. Staples Center

   d. Dignity Health Sports Park

10. The Dodgers have won a certain MLB award twice as many times as their nearest competitor, the New York Yankees, who have nine. What's the award in question?

    a. The Triple Crown

    b. The MVP

c. The Rookie of the Year

d. The Cy Young

11. In the decade of the 1960s, the Dodgers arguably achieved their greatest success with three NL pennants and two World Series wins. Which team did they beat in seven games in 1965 to capture the Series?

    a. The Boston Red Sox

    b. The Minnesota Twins

    c. The New York Yankees

    d. The San Francisco Giants

12. The decision by Branch Rickey to sign Jackie Robinson was a moral one (as well as a good business decision): The Methodist Church he belonged to was strongly in favor of "social justice."

    a. True

    b. False

13. Which of the following Dodgers stars was the youngest ever elected to the Hall of Fame?

    a. Duke Snider

    b. Pee Wee Reese

    c. Jackie Robinson

    d. Sandy Koufax

14. One Dodgers pitcher made MLB history by fanning more batters than the number of innings he pitched. Who was he?

    a. Jim Bunning

    b. Hideo Nomo

    c. Sandy Koufax

    d. Fernando Valenzuela

15. 1955 was the first year ever that an MVP was named in the World Series. Who was the Dodgers winner that unique year?

    a. Roy Campanella

    b. Don Newcombe

    c. Johnny Podres

    d. Jackie Robinson

16. On April 9, 1913, the Dodgers took their positions for the first time ever at Ebbets Field. Which opponent eked out a 1-0 win on that day?

    a. The Atlanta Braves

    b. The New York Highlanders

    c. The Philadelphia Phillies

    d. The Pittsburgh Pirates

17. In the early 19th century, the Dodgers were called the Robins. Why?

    a. They were named after a common northeastern bird.

    b. They were named after their manager, Wilbert Robinson.

    c. They were named after their manager, Wilhelm Robinhaut.

    d. They wore light blue uniforms that looked like a robin's egg.

18. Roger Kahn wrote a famous baseball book, "The Boys of Summer", about Brooklyn's 1955 Series victory, and those

players as they aged. What was the poetic phrase the book name came from?

    a. "the boys of summer in their ruin"

    b. "the boys and girls of summer on the beach"

    c. "the boys of summer grow long in the tooth"

    d. "the boys of summer never look back"

19. Which of the following players was one that Kahn's book did NOT track?

    a. Joe Black

    b. Roy Campanella

    c. Preacher Roe

    d. Larry Sherry

20. In only their second season in L.A., the Dodgers won the 1959 Series. Who was their opponent that year?

    a. The Chicago White Sox

    b. The Cleveland Indians

    c. The Detroit Tigers

    d. The Kansas City Royals

QUIZ ANSWERS

1. B — 1883

2. B — 6

3. A — 1945

4. D — The New York Giants

5. B — Ebbets Field

6. C — 7

7. D — He wanted to take advantage of MLB's lucrative expansion to the West Coast.

8. D — 1955

9. A — The L.A. Memorial Coliseum

10. C — The Rookie of the Year Award with 18

11. B — Minnesota Twins

12. A — True

13. D - Sandy Koufax

14. C - Sandy Koufax

15. C - Johnny Podres

16. C - The Philadelphia Phillies

17. B - They were named after their manager, Wilbert Robinson.

18. A - "the boys of summer in their ruin" (by Dylan Thomas)

19. D - Larry Sherry

20. A - The Chicago White Sox

DID YOU KNOW?

1. The signing of Jackie Robinson is still seen as a monumental turning point in the American Civil Rights movement, as well as in the overall integration of pro sports and the demise of the Negro Leagues.

2. In fact, the Dodgers` willingness to integrate when other teams declined to do it is seen as a key reason for their great success from 1947 to 1956, with Robinson, Don Newcombe and Roy Campanella leading the charge.

3. When the Brooklyn team started in the 1880s, they soon won the American Association championship in 1889. Then, in 1890, they reached new heights as pennant winners in the National League and "tied" the inter-league series against the Louisville Colonels.

4. As a result of the performance listed above, the Dodgers became the first team ever to win championships in different leagues in consecutive years, as well as the first pro baseball team to be broadcast on TV (1939), the first to wear batting helmets (1940) and the first to feature numbers on their uniform fronts (1952).

5. When Anita Martini, a sports journalist, was allowed to be the first female to enter a Major League Baseball locker room after the Dodgers won the pennant in 1974, the L.A. team also made history.

6.   The L.A. team also was the initial big-league team to make major inroads in various Asian countries, including Japan, South Korea and Taiwan. The Dodgers even built baseball fields in two Chinese cities. It was the first MLB club to establish an Asian office in 1998.

7.   The Dodgers count on their legions of L.A. fans and were the first team to beat the 3 million attendance mark in a single season in 1978. In fact, they did it six more times before any other team did it even once.

8.   During the 2011-2012 season, the high-profile divorce saga between the Dodgers owner at the time, Frank McCourt, and his wife, Jamie, hogged the headlines. Frank finally paid the cool sum of $131 million as part of the settlement to guarantee he'd continue as the team's owner.

9.   To honor the Dodgers' 50th anniversary in Los Angeles on March 29, 2008, the team played an exhibition game against the Boston Red Sox in the L.A. Memorial Coliseum, watched by a record-breaking crowd of 115,300. The game benefited the Dodgers charity, ThinkCure!, supporting children's cancer research.

10. Vin Scully announced Dodgers games on radio and TV from 1950 to 2016 and sometimes did as many as 100 broadcasts per season, mostly by himself. Of all people associated with the L.A. organization, he was voted by fans in 1976 as "the Most Memorable Personality" (on the field or off) in Dodgers history.

CHAPTER 2:

WHAT'S IN A NAME?

QUIZ TIME!

1. Way back in 1958, the Dodgers moved from the East Coast to the West Coast. What was the team's first-ever name?

    a. The Brooklyn Atlantics
    b. The Brooklyn Dodgers
    c. The Brooklyn Robins
    d. The Brooklyn Dodgeballers

2. When they became known as the Dodgers in 1895, there was a specific reason given for their dodging ability and hence the new team name. What was the motive?

    a. The original players were especially adept at stealing bases without being tagged out.
    b. The team was named after the many clever thieves or "dodgers" active in the city.
    c. When faster electric trolleys replaced horse-drawn ones in Brooklyn, citizens became adept at "dodging" them.

d. When cars first became popular in Brooklyn, pedestrians had to "dodge" them to stay alive.

3. The team had several names before finally settling on the Dodgers. Which one of the following was not one of them?

    a. The Bridegrooms
    b. The Grays
    c. The Greens
    d. The Superbas

4. At one point, the team was given the nickname "Dem Bums" for their less-than-stellar play. What was the reason?

    a. They signed numerous high-priced players, all of whom failed.
    b. They broke the record for most errors in three consecutive seasons.
    c. They lost to their cross-town rivals, the Yankees, on five occasions in 12 years.
    d. Their owners were likened to the real bums on Bleecker Street.

5. What was the name of the 1972 book that described in detail the Dodgers historic triumph over the Yankees in the 1955 World Series?

    a. The Brooklyn Babes
    b. The Boys of Summer
    c. The Endless Summer Boys
    d. The Brooklyn Word-Beaters

6. Wee Reese, from Ekron, KY, was a Dodgers cog from 1940 to 1958. He was also famous for his undying support of teammate Jackie Robinson, especially during the latter's first tough years. How did Reese earn his nickname?

   a. He was smaller and shorter than all his teammates growing up.
   b. He liked a specific kind of chocolate called the Pee Wee Bar.
   c. He was a champion marbles player ("pee wee" is a small marble).
   d. He was a champion horseshoe player ("pee wee" referred to a scoring "ringer").

7. While playing ball in a church league, Pee Wee Reese was noticed by the minor league Louisville Colonels' owner Cap Neal and soon became their shortstop. What nickname did he then inherit?

   a. The Little Colonel
   b. The Short Colonel
   c. The Colonel Captain
   d. The Magic Marble

8. Yet another reason given for the team being referred to as "Dem Bums" back in Brooklyn was the street character appearance of "the Artful Dodger," Jack Dawkins, in a Charles Dickens novel. What was the book in question?

   a. A Tale of Two Cities
   b. A Christmas Carol
   c. Oliver Twist
   d. The Pickwick Papers

9. When Mexican pitching ace Fernando Valenzuela graced the mound for the Dodgers in 1980, what was the name of the craze he caused?

   a. "Fernando Fever"
   b. "Mexican Madness"
   c. "The Valenzuela Vibe"
   d. "Fernandomania"

10. Since Valenzuela's velocity was limited, the Dodgers believed he needed to acquire another pitch. Which delivery did he learn from teammate Bobby Castillo?

   a. The forkball
   b. The knuckleball
   c. The screwball
   d. The slider

11. Hard-throwing pitcher Hideo Nomo is often credited as opening the MLB door for Japanese players. Before he debuted with the Dodgers in 1995, with whom did he play his first minor league game?

   a. The Modesto Nuts
   b. The Bakersfield Blaze
   c. The High Desert Mavericks
   d. The Portland Trailblazers

12. What contractual clause discovered by Nomo's agent, Don Nomura, allowed him to "escape" from Japanese baseball?

   a. The "Rule 5 Draft" clause (related to four years served in the minors)

b. The study-and-play-abroad clause

c. The voluntary retirement clause

d. The waiver request clause

13. Nomo's unique pitching windup and delivery (and fearsome forkball) took MLB by storm. What was he nicknamed as a result?

a. Nomo No-No

b. The Japanese Juggernaut

c. Tornado

d. Tsunami

14. Hot-hitting center fielder Edwin Donald Snider started in Brooklyn and accompanied the Dodgers out west. Which of the following was NOT one of his nicknames?

a. Duke

b. The Don of Flatland

c. The Duke of Flatbush

d. The Silver Fox

15. One Dodgers southpaw became famous not only for his pitching exploits but also for a special surgical procedure (also known as "ulnar collateral ligament reconstruction") that allowed him to recover from a serious arm injury. Who was he?

a. Don Drysdale

b. Orel Hershiser

c. Tommy John

d. Clayton Kershaw

16. Speed demon Maury Wills helped the Dodgers steal bases and win championships in the mid-1960s. With 104 stolen bags in 1962, whose record (that had stood since 1915) did Wills break?

    a. Lou Brock
    b. Ty Cobb
    c. Rickey Henderson
    d. Honus Wagner

17. The next time you go to Dodger Stadium for a game, it's guaranteed that you won't go hungry or thirsty. Besides the ubiquitous Dodger Dog, three of these food items are also available. Which is NOT (the last time we checked)?

    a. Brooklyn Dog
    b. Kirk Gibson's Gourmet Chicken Burger
    c. Plant Powered Burger
    d. West Is Best Double Burger

18. There's even a restaurant inside Dodgers Stadium called "Campy's Corner." Which renowned L.A. catcher is it named after?

    a. Bert Campaneris
    b. Roy Campanella
    c. Jim Campbell
    d. Clarence "Soup" Campbell

19. Ron Cey received a peculiar nickname from his college coach, Chuck "Bobo" Brayton, based on his slightly strange running motion. Which creature was his inspiration?

a. The Banana Slug
b. The Panther
c. The Penguin
d. The Platypus

20. Though they don't have their own mascot, the Dodgers borrowed the L.A. Kings' "Bailey" to show support for the city's hockey team in 2012. What does Bailey's uniform number 72 stand for?

   a. The average daily temperature (in degrees F.) in downtown L.A.
   b. The average daily number of miles of traffic jams in L.A.
   c. The average number of L.A. King wins in the last 10 seasons
   d. The last year the Dodgers won the World Series

QUIZ ANSWERS

1. A — The Brooklyn Atlantics

2. C — When faster electric trolleys replaced horse-drawn ones in Brooklyn, citizens became adept at "dodging" them.

3. C — The Greens

4. C — They lost to their cross-town rivals, the Yankees, on five occasions in 12 years.

5. B — "The Boys of Summer"

6. C — He was a champion marbles player ("pee wee" is a small marble).

7. A — The Little Colonel

8. C — Oliver Twist

9. D — "Fernandomania"

10. C — The screwball

11. B — The Bakersfield Blaze

12. C — The voluntary retirement clause

13. C — Tornado

14. B — The Don of Flatland

15. C — Tommy John

16. B — Ty Cobb

17. B — Kirk Gibson's Gourmet Chicken Burger

18. B — Roy Campanella

19. C — The Penguin

20. A — The average daily temperature (in degrees F.) in downtown L.A.

DID YOU KNOW?

1. The Los Angeles version of the Dodgers has existed since 1958, while the Brooklyn "Trolley Dodgers" name for the team lasted for only the 1911 and 1912 seasons.

2. Just before the club made the move to the National League in 1889, the team was christened the Brooklyn Bridegrooms because six players had coincidentally wed during the 1888 season.

3. Both the Dodgers and Giants had their humble origins in the metropolis of New York. They also both went west following the 1957 season, thus transplanting their rivalry to the two biggest cities on the West Coast, Los Angeles and San Francisco.

4. The Brooklyn teams of the late '20s became known as the "Daffiness Boys" because of their distracted style of error-ridden play. Once they even had two men declared out at the same base, while a third was ruled safe. Those responsible for this base-running "brilliance" were Dazzy Vance, Chick Fewster and Babe Herman.

5. When Leland "Larry" MacPhail was named Dodgers general manager in 1938, he was already known for introducing night games with the Reds. He renovated Ebbets Field, brought in Cincinnati's radio announcer Red Barber, and quickly went about breaking the New York executives' agreement banning live baseball broadcasts.

6. Branch Rickey revolutionized baseball by signing Jackie Robinson and cracking the so-called "color barrier." Rickey apparently saw his chance to even the playing field when Commissioner Kenesaw Mountain Landis, an arch-segregationist, died in 1944.

7. Knowing that Robinson would have to stand up to boos and taunts as the first-ever African-American MLB player, Rickey considered Jackie's outstanding baseball skills, personal character, UCLA education and rank as captain in the U.S. Army.

8. When the Jacksonville (FL) city government, citing segregation laws, refused to allow a Dodgers exhibition game featuring Robinson in 1946, Daytona Beach stepped up to host. To this day, you can find Jackie Robinson Ballpark (changed from City Island Ballpark) there, though the team actually trained at Vero Beach till 2008.

9. With Robinson in the lineup, along with three-time MVP Roy Campanella, Cy Young Award winner Don Newcombe, Jim Gilliam, and Joe Black, the Dodgers won six of 10 pennants from 1947 to 1956. Robinson was the first African-American elected into the Hall of Fame in 1962.

10. When Los Angeles city officials attended the World Series in 1956, their original target to entice west was the Washington Senators, who ended up moving to Bloomington, Minnesota in 1961 and became the Minnesota Twins.

CHAPTER 3:

FAMOUS QUOTES

QUIZ TIME!

1. The Dodgers won pennants in 1941, 1947, 1949, 1952, and 1953 but lost in the Series each time to the Yankees, so they become known as "Dem Bums." What was the fans' lamentable phrase at the time?

    a. "Better luck next time"
    b. "Dem bums'll never win"
    c. "Next year, the Yanks will be yesteryear"
    d. "Wait 'til next year"

2. The Dodgers had a popular organist in Brooklyn named Ms. Gooding, who pleased fans with her playing until the Dodgers moved west. The supporters went as far as to say she was "the only Dodger who played every game without an error." What was her first name?

    a. Gail
    b. Gladys
    c. Gloria
    d. Harriet

3. Floyd Caves "Babe" Herman suited up for the Brooklyn team when they were still called the Robins in the 1920s. His dangerous bat kept him in the lineup. In fact, his 1931 teammate, Fresco Thompson, quipped, "He wore a glove for one reason: because it was a league _____."

   a. custom
   b. habit
   c. recommendation
   d. rule

4. On August 15, 1926, with one out and the bases full, Herman ripped a double against the Boston Braves and tried to stretch it into a triple. Unfortunately, when he got to third base, teammates Chick Fewster and Dazzy Vance were already there. Vance was entitled to the base, having arrived first, but Fewster and Herman were both tagged out. The next day, the joke began: "The Dodgers have three men on base." What was the retort?

   a. "Nice! We're losing by four runs…."
   b. "Great! Can one of them please score?"
   c. "Oh, yeah? Which base?"
   d. "That's usually called a triple play."

5. The 1934 NL race came down to the final games of the season. The Brooklyn Dodgers, in sixth place at the time, acted as spoilers, beating the New York Giants, thus giving St. Louis the pennant. It was revenge for the Dodgers because Giants manager Bill Terry had asked if Brooklyn was "still in the league" at the season's start. Who was the Dodgers manager then?

a. Casey Stengel

b. Frankie Frisch

c. Jimmie Wilson

d. Pie Traynor

6. Jackie Robinson affirmed the right of every American to first-class citizenship and backed it up with his stellar play for the Dodgers. He once said, "Life is not a _____ sport. If you're going to spend your whole life in the grandstand just watching what goes on, in my opinion you're wasting your life."

a. contact

b. simple

c. spectator

d. violent

7. What two words complete the following Jackie Robinson quote? "I never cared about _____ as much as I cared about _____."

a. acceptance/respect

b. the Giants/the Dodgers

c. love/liberty

d. money/honesty

8. Vin Scully, the Dodgers' voice for a mere 67 years, filled the airwaves with anecdotes and colorful quips about his team. Upon hearing that an L.A. slugger had a bruised knee and was listed as "day-to-day," he quipped, "Aren't we all?" Who was the Dodgers player?

a. Andre Dawson

b. Andre Ethier

c. Adrián González

d. André the Giant

9. Many were amazed that Vin Scully did what he did for as long as he did, and all while "bleeding Dodger blue." In the end, he said, "It's only me." Which of the following roles did he leave out of that classic quote?

a. "I'm not a military general."

b. "I'm not a business guru."

c. "I'm not the king of the world."

d. "I'm not a philosopher or author."

10. Before becoming vice president and later president of the Brooklyn club, Lee MacPhail was recommended for the Reds' GM position by Branch Rickey. Responsible for numerous innovations, including players flying to away games, MacPhail came with a caveat from Rickey:

a. He was "the straw that stirred the drink."

b. He was "not the best manager in the world, but he'll bring home the bacon."

c. He was known to "stay out late, but show up early."

d. He was "a wild man at times, but he'll do the job."

11. One Dodgers manager had a testy relationship with MacPhail, and was heard to say of his boss: "There's a thin line between genius and insanity and, in Larry's case, it was so thin you could see him drifting back and forth." Who was the man?

a. Walter Alston

b. Leo Durocher

c. Tommy Lasorda

d. Joe Torre

12. Leo Durocher, also known as "Leo the Lip" and "Lippy," was no stranger to controversy as the Dodgers manager starting in the late 1930s. He was notorious for instructing his pitchers to "bean" opposing batters. What was his specific order?

   a. "Stick it to him any time!"

   b. "You may now hit that batter!"

   c. "Stick it in his ear!"

   d. "Stick it where the sun don't shine!"

13. Durocher made no bones about his lack of love for umpires in general. He was heard to say, "I never questioned the integrity of an umpire. Their _____, yes."

   a. education

   b. eyesight

   c. knowledge

   d. salary

14. Once upon a time, did Durocher really say the following, "You argue with the umpire because there is nothing else you can do about it"?

   a. True

   b. False

15. In what way did "Leo the Lip" liken the great game of baseball to going to church?

    a. "Both are equally mysterious."
    b. "You don't always see God, or the Dodgers win. But tomorrow's a new day."
    c. "You pay very little, and sometimes you're saved."
    d. "Many attend, few understand."

16. Walter Alston, manager of the Dodgers from 1954 to 1976, signed 23 one-year contracts to stick with the club. A bit less effusive than Durocher, he was known as "the Quiet Man." Who was the one player who made Alston wish he hadn't become a manager?

    a. Hank Aaron
    b. Mickey Mantle
    c. Willie Mays
    d. Roger Maris

17. Alston often said he didn't worry too much about winning "a whole bunch (of games) in a row." He preferred to win a few, and then lose one, and things would even out. How did he say he put himself through college?

    a. Betting on baseball
    b. Playing pool
    c. Shining other students' shoes
    d. Waiting on tables

18. Walter Alston also stressed the importance of living (and managing) in "the now." What was one thing he worried about, and another he didn't?

a. Tomorrow's weather & climate change

b. Paying the bills & saving for a rainy day

c. Tomorrow's game & next year's job

d. Listening to his players & learning from other coaches

19. Continuing in a long line of top Dodgers managers, Tommy Lasorda was at the L.A. helm for 20 years starting in 1976. One mentor taught Tommy that "a pat on a shoulder can be just as important as a kick in the butt." Who was the elder coach?

a. Jimmy Collins

b. Ralph Houk

c. Casey Stengel

d. Yogi Berra

20. As always in baseball, the Dodgers under Lasorda were accused of cheating. Tommy responded simply, "No, we don't cheat." How did he finish the phrase?

a. "And even if we did, I'd never tell you."

b. "Everybody's just jealous of a winner."

c. "I admit I once cheated playing poker. But baseball? Never!"

d. "Cheating's for cheaters. All we are is winners."

QUIZ ANSWERS

1. D — "Wait 'til next year"

2. B — Gladys

3. A — custom

4. C — "Oh, yeah? Which base?"

5. A — Casey Stengel

6. C — spectator

7. A — acceptance/respect

8. A — Andre Dawson

9. C — "I'm not the king of the world."

10. D — He was "a wild man at times, but he'll do the job."

11. B — Leo Durocher

12. C — "Stick it in his ear!"

13. B — eyesight

14. A — True

15. D — "Many attend, few understand."

16. A — Hank Aaron

17. B — Playing pool

18. C — Tomorrow's game / next year's job

19. B — Ralph Houk

20. A — "And even if we did, I'd never tell you."

DID YOU KNOW?

1. Tommy Lasorda played briefly for the Triple-A Denver Bears for skipper Ralph Houk. Lasorda later admitted that Houk had a huge influence on his managing style. "Ralph taught me that if you treat players like human beings, they will play like Superman," he claimed in his biography, *I Live For This: Baseball's Last True Believer*.

2. For all of us "burned out" by the C-virus pandemic, Lasorda had the eternal answer: "Guys ask me, don't I get burned out? How can you get burned out doing something you love? I ask you, have you ever got tired of kissing a pretty girl?"

3. Lasorda used his extensive experience navigating the L.A. freeway system to distill the essence of the sport he adored. "Baseball is like driving, it's the one who gets home safely that counts."

4. Game 1 of the 1988 World Series: The Dodgers batting in the bottom of the ninth against future Hall-of-Famer Dennis Eckersley of the Oakland A's. Hobbled L.A. star Kirk Gibson was told to grab a bat, and the rest is history. Vin Scully narrated, "3-and-2. Sax waiting on deck. But the game right now is at the plate. High fly ball into right field, she is gone! In a year that has been so improbable, the impossible has happened. And now the only question was whether he could make it around the base paths unassisted?"

5. An All-American wide receiver at Michigan State, Gibson brought his toughness to baseball. In the 1984 Series, he hit another colossal blast off Goose Gossage, who had refused to walk him with a base open. "My idea of a 'super bowl' is when the catcher is standing in front of the plate with the ball, waiting for me as I round third ... and I make him drop it. That's a quality Super Bowl," Gibby said.

6. After he retired from playing, Gibson moved into management and then broadcasting with the Detroit Tigers. Here's his take on running a ball club: "If you're a manager, you can't get frustrated and be emotional. You have to continue to steer the ship, you can't let go of the wheel, because who knows where it will go then?"

7. Orel "Bulldog" Hershiser put up some sparkling pitching stats in 1988 and beyond for L.A., including 59 straight innings without giving up a run. Orel even admitted that a little luck helped: "No matter how noble and special people want to make the playoffs out to be ... it's a crapshoot."

8. In one particularly bad outing, manager Tommy Lasorda lashed into Hershiser for being too timid and giving hitters too much respect. Teammates later referred to the lambasting by Lasorda as "the sermon on the mound."

9. Hershiser stretched his career with the Indians, Giants and Mets. One of the reasons was his "palette" of pitches and more precise delivery as he got longer in the tooth. Orel stressed, "You'll hear pitchers say, 'I had great stuff and

got shelled,' but you never hear them say, 'I had great location and got shelled.'"

10. Dodgers star Steve Garvey summed up his feelings (and those of many Dodgers and Padres fans) by saying, "I have been blessed to win a number of awards and been involved in numerous historical baseball moments over my 20-year career with the L.A. Dodgers and San Diego Padres."

CHAPTER 4:

DODGER RECORDS

QUIZ TIME!

1. Back in 1884, the Brooklyn Bridegrooms averaged 1,194 spectators per game. What did the 2019 version of the L.A. Dodgers average in per-game attendance?

    a. 42,755

    b. 45,342

    c. 49,066

    d. 52,177

2. The winningest manager in the Dodgers' distinguished history is Walter "Smokey" Alston. How many games did he win in his 22-year stint?

    a. 1,880 games

    b. 2,040 games

    c. 2,122 games

    d. 2,404 games

3. Zachariah Davis Wheat, also affectionately known as "Zack" or "Buck" (and brother of Mack Wheat), born in

1888, leads one Dodgers statistical category by far. What is it?

   a. .352 batting average

   b. 379 home runs

   c. .573 slugging percentage

   d. 8,859 at-bats

4. Gary Sheffield set several Dodgers batting records, some 100 years after Zack Wheat. Which of the following did he NOT break?

   a. On-base percentage (.424)

   b. On-base plus slugging percentage (.998)

   c. Slugging percentage (.573)

   d. Home runs (379)

5. Maury Wills stole 490 bases as an Artful Dodger, but he was also caught in the attempt 171 times. Who was the L.A. player who bested Wills in stolen base percentage?

   a. Yasiel Puig

   b. Davey Lopes

   c. Mike Piazza

   d. Steve Sax

6. The Dodgers have a knack of hauling in great rookies, including the winners of four straight Rookie of the Year awards from 1979 to 1982. Which of the following players was NOT among them?

   a. Rick Sutcliffe

   b. Steve Howe

c. Fernando Valenzuela

d. Eric Karros

7. When Fernando Valenzuela won the Rookie of the Year Award in 1981, he created fan and media mania by completing each one of his first eight starts. How many of them were shutouts?

a. 3

b. 4

c. 5

d. 6

8. Not only was Jackie Robinson the first African-American athlete to play pro baseball, but he was a vocal civil rights activist. He refused to move to the back of a segregated army bus and was court-martialed but acquitted. For which semi-pro team did he play football before joining the Dodgers?

a. The Chicago Bears

b. The Honolulu Bears

c. The Midway Monsters

d. The Waikiki Wave Riders

9. Matthew, Robinson's older brother, inspired Jackie to pursue his athletic dreams. In what event did the brother finish just behind Jesse Owens in the 1936 Berlin Olympics?

a. The 100-meter dash

b. The 200-meter dash

c. The 110-meter high hurdles

d. The pentathlon

10. Despite facing racism in the form of insults and even death threats, Robinson made it to the big leagues. What was the first otherwise all-white farm team he played for in 1946?

    a. The Maine Black Bears
    b. The Montreal Expos
    c. The Montreal Royals
    d. The Abilene Blue Sox

11. Even Robinson's teammates sometimes refused to take the field with him. What did manager Leo Durocher crack back to get them to join Jackie on the diamond?

    a. He said he'd sooner trade them than Robinson.
    b. He said their pay might find its way into Robinson's account, not theirs.
    c. He promised them extra practice at 6 AM on Sunday.
    d. He informed them that racists on his team always ran more sprints.

12. While Robinson was being harassed by fans, what simple gesture did Dodgers captain Pee Wee Reese make that resonated in the baseball world and beyond?

    a. He put his finger to his lips to silence the fans.
    b. He offered to carry Robinson's bat and glove.
    c. He walked over and put his arm around Robinson.
    d. He gave Robinson a pair of Bose headphones to put on.

13. During the 1949 season, Jackie started to win some fans over with a .342 batting average, a stolen base crown, and the National League's MVP Award. What song was written to celebrate his success?

    a. "Jackie Robinson's Coming to Town!"
    b. "Did You See Jackie Robinson Hit That Ball?"
    c. "Hey Jackie!"
    d. "The Jackie Robinson Stolen Base Shuffle"

14. 1953 was a vintage year in Brooklyn in terms of wins and winning percentage. The 2017 gang in L.A. almost equaled both marks. What were the two numbers for the latter team?

    a. 98 wins/.630
    b. 100 wins/.632
    c. 104 wins/.642
    d. 110 wins/.666

15. Though there are no set rules for retiring club numbers, generally all the players whose numbers were retired played mostly for the Dodgers and became Hall-of-Famers. Who was the notable exception?

    a. Don Drysdale
    b. Jim Gilliam
    c. Sandy Koufax
    d. Don Sutton

16. Two Dodgers stars, both big award winners, did not have their numbers retired because they never got into the Hall

of Fame. Which of them, Fernando Valenzuela or Steve Garvey, hasn't had his number (34) worn since leaving L.A. in 1991?

    a. Fernando Valenzuela

    b. Steve Garvey

17. Don Sutton could really blow the ball by them as a Dodgers pitcher from 1966 to 1980. He holds almost every pitching record for the team. In 550 games overall, how many shutouts did he toss?

    a. 41

    b. 48

    c. 52

    d. 60

18. Back in the early Brooklyn days (from 1892 to 1901), William Park Kennedy was a dominant pitcher who set team records for complete games (280) and walks (1,130). What was his nickname?

    a. "Brickyard"

    b. "Junkyard Dog"

    c. "Complete Game Kennedy"

    d. "William The Walk Master"

19. In 1884, a Brooklyn pitcher with the last name of Terry put up some Herculean numbers with 55 starts, 54 complete games, and 35 losses. What was his first name?

    a. Adonis

    b. Apollo

c. Titan

d. Zeus

20. The current Dodgers have a consecutive postseason appearance streak of seven. Only two other teams (with 14 and 13 respectively) have done better. Which teams are they?

    a. The Atlanta Braves and N.Y. Yankees

    b. The Baltimore Orioles and Boston Red Sox

    c. The St. Louis Cardinals and Milwaukee Brewers

    d. The San Francisco Giants and Chicago White Sox

QUIZ ANSWERS

1. C — 49,066

2. B — 2,040 games

3. D — 8,859 at-bats

4. D — 379 home runs / Duke Snider

5. B — Davey Lopes / 83.1%

6. D — Eric Karros won in 1992.

7. C — 5

8. B — The Honolulu Bears

9. B — The 200-meter dash

10. C — The Montreal Royals

11. A — He said he'd sooner trade them than Robinson.

12. C — He walked over and put his arm around Robinson.

13. B — "Did You See Jackie Robinson Hit That Ball?"

14. C — 104 wins/ .642 (The Dodgers finally broke the '53 record with 106 wins in 2019.)

15. B — Jim Gilliam

16. A — Fernando Valenzuela

17. C — 52

18. A — "Brickyard"

19. A — Adonis

20. A — The Atlanta Braves and New York Yankees

DID YOU KNOW?

1. The book title *The Boys of Summer"* refers to the original 1953 Dodgers super team, including Robinson, Roy Campanella, Gil Hodges, and Duke Snider, that cruised to 105 victories in 154 games. It took the 2019 squad 162 games, but they broke the record with 106 wins.

2. The 2019 team cruised to the NL West title for the seventh straight season, finishing a division-record 21 games ahead of the second-place Arizona Diamondbacks.

3. William Henry O'Kelleher Jr. (who later "Americanized" his name to Keeler), batting for Brooklyn in 1899, set an MLB record with only two strikeouts in 570 at-bats. His advice to teammates was simple: "Keep your eye clear, and hit 'em where they ain't."

4. At 5 feet 4½, Keeler had a phenomenal 206 singles in the 1898 season, a record that stood until it was beaten by Ichiro Suzuki more than 100 years later.

5. After a stint with the Sioux Falls Packers in South Dakota, Don Sutton debuted for the Dodgers in 1966. He had 1,354 career at-bats without hitting a home run. Sutton also threw nine scoreless innings in a game without earning a decision seven times in his career.

6. Another Dodger Don, in this case Drysdale, was called "Big D." He formed a dynamic pitching duo with Sandy

Koufax in the 1950s and '60s. He didn't shy away from brushback pitches, and his Dodgers record of 154 hit batsmen still stands. He also batted .300 and hit seven homers during his MVP season in 1965.

7. Sanford "Sandy" Koufax pitched 12 years for the Dodgers before retiring after the 1966 season because of arthritis in his pitching arm. Only six years later, at the age of 36, he became the youngest ever player elected to the Baseball Hall of Fame.

8. Duke Snider handled a heavy bat for the Dodgers and led the NL in fielding average as a center fielder on three occasions. He holds the franchise's career record for most intentional walks with 141.

9. Zack Greinke battled anxiety and depression but made it in the big leagues. Some of his blues lifted when he signed with the Dodgers for $147 million in 2012. He started the 2014 season by extending his streak of giving up less than 2 earned runs to 22 straight games, an MLB record.

10. Few major leaguers come from Curaçao, but Kenley Jansen crossed various oceans to play with the Gulf Coast Dodgers, Ogden Raptors, West Oahu CaneFires and Great Lakes Loons as a catcher before making a switch to pitcher and reaching the big leagues. He led the NL with 41 saves and pitched "an immaculate inning" (recording three strikeouts on nine pitches) in 2017.

CHAPTER 5:

HOW ABOUT A TRADE?

QUIZ TIME!

1. The Dodgers acquired Dazzy Vance from the minor league New Orleans Pelicans in 1922. He proceeded to win 18 games as a rookie and made it to the Hall of Fame. How old was he when he signed?

    a. 28

    b. 31

    c. 35

    d. 39

2. When the Dodgers acquired Pee Wee Reese from Boston in 1939, he became team captain, a key Jackie Robinson ally and a Hall-of-Famer. In *The Boys of Summer*, what reason did writer Roger Kahn give for the trade?

    a. Reese played the same position as then Red Sox player/manager Joe Cronin.

    b. Reese couldn't adjust to the hard Boston winters.

    c. Reese's bat went stone cold in Boston.

d. Red Sox player/manager Joe Cronin and Reese had an argument in the dugout.

3. L.A. traded for Andy Messersmith with their cross-town rivals the Angels in 1972. Andy pitched well enough, but he's remembered more for something he did off the diamond. What was it?

a. He became an arbitrator in his free time and helped many Dodgers.
b. He challenged the reserve clause in arbitration, opening the door to free agency.
c. He married a Hollywood superstar.
d. He participated in numerous charity golf events while a Dodger.

4. Catcher Mike Piazza was a darling Dodger until his agent got embroiled in a trade dispute with a studio exec running a baseball team behind the GM's back. With what team's cap did Mike enter the Hall of Fame?

a. The Florida Marlins
b. The New York Mets
c. The New York Yankees
d. The Philadelphia Phillies

5. The player from Florida who replaced Piazza slammed the ball all over Chavez Ravine and was a two-time All-Star for the Dodgers. But he couldn't make fans forget a badly-timed trade that shouldn't have happened. Who was that player?

a. Bobby Bonilla

b. Charles Johnson

c. Jim Eisenreich

d. Gary Sheffield

6. After Atlanta traded away his mentor, Dusty Baker wanted to go back west, closer to his hometown of Riverside. His first L.A. season in 1976 was rough, but he settled down as a two-time All-Star, Gold Glove winner, and a participant in three Series. Who was the mentor?

a. Buzz Capra

b. Cito Gaston

c. Hank Aaron

d. Phil Niekro

7. It's not easy to give up a future Cy Young Award winner like Bob Welch. But the Dodgers traded him for the pieces that helped them win the Series in 1988. Which of the following players did they NOT get in the three-team trade?

a. Alfredo Griffin

b. Jay Howell

c. Jesse Orosco

d. Mike Scioscia

8. Los Angeles acquired Manny Ramirez from the Red Sox in a three-team swap in 2008. Manny managed to play three months, batting .533 in the NL Championship Series, until he was tainted in a PED scandal. What did he rake in from his two-year deal?

a. $10 million
b. $25 million
c. $45 million
d. $106 million

9. In 2012, the Dodgers showed they meant business by spending big. They went after Adrián González and Carl Crawford from Boston, among others. The Los Angeles payroll for the 2013 season ended up at a quarter billion dollars.

   a. True
   b. False

10. A Christmas present in December 2018, for Yasiel Puig and Matt Kemp, both long-term spark plugs for the Dodgers, was a trade to the Reds. Who arrived and then turned out to be a key to the 2020 Mookie Betts swap?

    a. Homer Bailey
    b. Jeter Downs
    c. Kyle Farmer
    d. Josiah Gray

11. The Dodgers traded for Mookie Betts in 2020, hoping the former Boston star could take them to the promised land. What other player came as well?

    a. Rubby De La Rosa
    b. Connor Wong
    c. David Price
    d. Alex Verdugo

12. Soon after ex-Red Sox Mookie arrived, COVID-19 closed baseball down. Fans felt a bit more secure about him staying when Betts said, "It didn't take long to get used to (L.A.), the guys in there made it so seamless. It was like ____."

    a. heaven
    b. home
    c. heck
    d. nirvana

13. Some pundits say that the worst trade in Dodgers' history was when Pedro Martinez was shipped to the Montreal Expos in 1993. Who came in exchange?

    a. Delino DeShields
    b. Brett Butler
    c. Pedro Astacio
    d. Raúl Mondesi

14. In 1994, infielder Jody Reed was offered $7.8 million by L.A. for three years, with a base of $2 million. However, his agent thought he could snag $11 million in the market. Which team ended up giving Jody $750K for the first year?

    a. The California Angels
    b. The Milwaukee Brewers
    c. The Oakland Athletics
    d. The Texas Rangers

15. Ron Fairly played for the Dodgers and several other teams. All told, he participated in over 7,000 MLB games,

both as a player and broadcaster. Why was he traded from L.A. to Montreal in 1969?

    a. He was involved in several brawls, on the field and off.

    b. He broke five bats in as many games.

    c. He went hitless in 30 straight games.

    d. His batting average dipped to .219.

16. Along with Manny Mota, the Dodgers acquired Maurice "Maury" Wills in the Ron Fairly deal. What was Maury's middle name?

    a. Maverick

    b. Messiah

    c. Milton

    d. Morning

17. After the arrival of Wills, the Dodgers pumped up their offensive firepower. What was Maury mainly credited with?

    a. His constant hustle was an inspiration to teammates

    b. His heavy weightlifting allowed him to hit for more power

    c. Reviving the stolen base as an offensive tactic

    d. Reviving stolen signs as an overall tactic

18. When Jim Murray started to write for the *Los Angeles Times* in the 1960s, players wanted to be traded to the Dodgers. Which of the following was NOT one of the reasons?

a. Their beautiful stadium

b. The huge crowds

c. Their private plane

d. The relatively low humidity

19. When L.A. went after the Angels' Andy Messersmith again in 1972, they traded five players, including one who became MLB's first African-American manager. Who was he?

a. Dusty Baker

b. Riccardo Ingram

c. Frank Robinson

d. Dave Roberts

20. When Frank Robinson was traded from L.A. to the Angels at age 37, he moved from the National League to the American League. What rule helped him to keep his career alive?

a. The Bases-Loaded Rule

b. The Designated Hitter Rule

c. The Full Count Rule

d. The Extra Inning Rule

QUIZ ANSWERS

1. B — 31

2. A — Reese played the same position as then Red Sox player/manager Joe Cronin.

3. B — He challenged the reserve clause in arbitration, opening the door to free agency.

4. B — The New York Mets

5. D — Gary Sheffield

6. C — Hank Aaron

7. D — Mike Scioscia

8. C — $45 million

9. A — True

10. B — Jeter Downs

11. C — David Price

12. B — home

13. A — Delino DeShields

14. B — The Milwaukee Brewers

15. D — His batting average dipped to .219.

16. D — Morning

17. C — Reviving the stolen base as an offensive tactic

18. D — The relatively low humidity

19. C — Frank Robinson

20. B — The Designated Hitter Rule

DID YOU KNOW?

1. When the Dodgers traded for Andy Messersmith, they almost included a young third baseman with "an erratic arm and uncertain bat." But they kept Steve Garvey, turned him into a first baseman, and he hit the lights out.

2. That trade with the cross-town Angels was such a big deal that the L.A. Times ran an editorial that said, "If you get burned in a deal by the Pirates, they'll be laughing at you in Pittsburgh. Not so if a team 25 miles away undresses you. You may then expect to be kept in constant awareness of your cerebral nudity."

3. In 60 years of rivalry, there have only been 15 deals between the Dodgers and the Angels. Six involved only the sale of a player's contract.

4. In 1967, an infielder named John Werhas was shipped from the Dodgers to the Angels. As a player, he had little impact on either team, but he joined a ministry and served as a chaplain in both clubhouses.

5. When Adrián González was abruptly traded to L.A. from Boston together with Josh Beckett (the deal also included $11 million in cash), he bashed a three-run homer against Miami in his first Dodgers at-bat.

6. In 2017, the Dodgers decided to trade Adrián González to the Atlanta Braves for Matt Kemp. Right away, the Braves

designated González for assignment and he was promptly released. Adrián had to give up his no-trade clause to make the deal happen and become a free agent.

7. When Kemp came back to L.A. in the aforementioned deal, the Dodgers were relieved of some dodgy contracts, allowing the team to slide under the $197 million luxury tax threshold.

8. González tweeted his thanks to "the Dodger Nation" (after having played previously for "the Red Sox Nation"). Adrián had already accepted a limited role on the bench due to the hot bat of Cody Bellinger, the regular first baseman. "Lifting the no-trade clause is the hardest decision I have ever made in my career due to the fact that I loved every single second being a Dodger."

9. What were some of the Dodgers' worst deals? They gave up Gary Sheffield in 2002 and he hit 25-plus homers five more times and drove in 120+ runs in three more seasons.

10. When Tommy Lasorda served briefly as general manager, he plugged a hole in the bullpen by unloading a young Paul Konerko for closer Jeff Shaw. Though Jeff pitched well, Konerko clocked the ball all over the diamond for the Chicago White Sox and was a six-time All-Star.

CHAPTER 6:

CHAT ABOUT STATS

QUIZ TIME!

1. Not every hitter can hammer home runs all the time. Which two Dodgers are career leaders in sacrifice hits and sacrifice flies?

   a. Pee Wee Reese & Duke Snider

   b. Jake Daubert & Eric Karros

   c. Cody Bellinger & Gary Sheffield

   d. Willie Keeler & Zack Wheat

2. Carl Furillo, also called "The Reading Rifle" because of his strong, accurate arm, leads the Dodgers in one dubious offensive category. What was it?

   a. Caught stealing

   b. Double plays grounded into

   c. Outs made

   d. Strikeouts

3. Speaking of Furillo and his rifle-like arm, he recorded 10 or more assists in nine straight seasons (leading the league

twice) from 1947 to 1959 and he retired with the fifth most games ever in right field in the NL. How many?

   a. 1,177
   b. 1,256
   c. 1,362
   d. 1,409

4. Though Walter Alston had a long stretch of success as the L.A. manager, his major league playing career was notoriously short. How long was it?

   a. One out, no at-bats, with the Chicago Cubs in 1936
   b. Two innings played, one at-bat, with the St. Louis Cardinals in 1936
   c. Two games played, four at-bats, with the St. Louis Cardinals in 1936
   d. Two weeks played, 6 at-bats, with the Chicago Cubs in 1936

5. Before Alston made it to the majors, he had a short stint in 1946 as skipper of one notable minor league team. What was that team's claim to fame?

   a. The Nashua Dodgers were the first racially integrated pro team in the U.S.
   b. The Nashua Dodgers were the first pro team to go an entire season unbeaten.
   c. The New York Black Yankees were the first racially integrated pro team in the U.S.
   d. The Boston Colored Giants were the first racially integrated pro team in the U.S.

6. Clayton "the Claw" Kershaw recorded two sub-2.00 ERA seasons in 2013 and 2014 before he broke the previous salary mark for all players. How much did he haul in?

   a. $22 million a year
   b. $27 million a year
   c. $30 million a year
   d. $36 million a year

7. When Sandy Koufax signed to pitch with the Dodgers at the tender age of 19, he was termed a "bonus baby." Why?

   a. His bonus was the highest ever paid at the time to a player younger than 20.
   b. He wasn't allowed to touch his bonus money until age 21.
   c. He was required to spend his first two years in the majors.
   d. He was required to spend his first year in the bullpen.

8. Though he only boasted a 36-40 pitching record in his first six years, Koufax matched one record previously set by Bob Feller. What was it?

   a. 18 strikeouts in a game
   b. 22 strikeouts in a game
   c. 6 assists by a pitcher in a game
   d. 4 runners picked off in a game

9. In 1965, Sandy Koufax's sterling stats included 382 strikeouts. Which pitcher finally broke his record in 1973?

   a. Steve Carlton

b. Randy Jones

c. Pedro Martinez

d. Nolan Ryan

10. Koufax had 8 World Series pitching appearances – though he won only 4 of 7 starts – before his relatively early retirement at age 30. What was his stellar ERA in those games?

a. 0.61

b. 0.73

c. 0.95

d. 1.15

11. Koufax's counterpart, Don Drysdale, was more comfortable in the L.A. spotlight (after all, he was born in La-La Land). Later in his career, his teammates were anemic at the plate and Don's batting average was higher than that of any position player. What was it?

a. .280

b. .292

c. .300

d. .315

12. According to Drysdale, the most impressive run he ever had was six straight shutouts along with 58.2 scoreless innings in 1968. The run was so spectacular that opponents accused him of throwing the spitter. Did he ever admit it?

a. Yes

b. No

13. Dazzy Vance's year in 1924 broke just about every pitching record. He went 28-6 with a 2.16 ERA and whiffed 262 batters, almost double the mark of his teammate. Who was that Dodger?

    a. Wilbert Robinson
    b. Johnny Frederick
    c. Burleigh Grimes
    d. Rogers Hornsby

14. "Dazzy Vance could throw a cream puff through a battleship," said Dodgers teammate Johnny Frederick. What was Vance's MVP award accompanied by in 1924?

    a. $1,000 in gold coins
    b. A Model-T Ford car
    c. $1,000 in gold bars
    d. A free trip across the Brooklyn Bridge

15. Dodger Stadium, also referred to as "Blue Heaven on Earth," is the largest existing baseball stadium in terms of seat capacity. It's also the oldest such structure west of the Mississippi River. Which of the following is not older?

    a. Boston's Fenway Park
    b. Chicago's Wrigley Field
    c. Cincinnati's Riverfront Stadium
    d. Old Yankee Stadium

16. The construction of Dodger Stadium in 1962 cost $23 million. What would be the equivalent dollar cost in 2018?

    a. $124 million

b. $164 million

c. $189 million

d. $234 million

17. After a 10-year struggle, "the Battle of Chavez Ravine," between the city and residents trying to keep their property, the stadium was built. How heavy were some of the precast concrete units used?

a. 10 tons

b. 18 tons

c. 26 tons

d. 32 tons

18. Former Dodgers owner Frank McCourt, always a mover and shaker, used Dodger Stadium as collateral for a loan to repay another loan from another former owner, News Corporation. How much was the later loan?

a. $150 million

b. $200 million

c. $250 million

d. $300 million

19. In 2008, the L.A. City Council voted to give Dodger Stadium and environs its very own zip code, 90090. Bounded by three streets, what was the new area called?

a. Dodger Downs

b. Dodger Dome

c. Dodgertown

d. Dodgerville

20. Directly behind Dodger Stadium's home plate, a large elevator rises to the uppermost seats and bears a giant L.A. logo. How many stories high is the elevator?

    a. 6
    b. 8
    c. 10
    d. 12

QUIZ ANSWERS

1. B — Jake Daubert & Eric Karros

2. B — Double plays grounded into

3. D — 1,408

4. B — Two innings played, one at-bat, with the St. Louis Cardinals in 1936

5. A — The Nashua (NH) Dodgers were the first integrated pro team in the U.S.

6. C — $30 million a year

7. C — He was required to spend his first two years in the majors.

8. A — 18 strikeouts in a game

9. D — Nolan Ryan (383 strikeouts)

10. C — 0.95

11. C — .300

12. A — Yes

13. C — Burleigh Grimes

14. A — $1,000 in gold coins

15. C — Cincinnati's Riverfront Stadium

16. C — $189 million

17. D — 32 tons

18. C — $250 million

19. C — Dodgertown

20. C — 10

DID YOU KNOW?

1. In 2017, to celebrate the 70th anniversary of Jackie Robinson's big-league debut, the Dodgers unveiled an 800-pound (360 kg) sculpture of the rookie sliding into home plate.

2. Southern California tends to be a bit dry. Before a rainout in 1976, the only Los Angeles Dodgers game rained out was against St. Louis on April 21, 1967. The 1976 rainout ended a streak of 724 games without postponement. No rainouts occurred between April 1988 and April 1999, an ML record of 856 games that has been eclipsed by the Dodgers' current run of no rainouts.

3. Dodger Stadium had never had the opportunity to host a Game 7 of any playoff series until the 1988 NLCS. The Dodgers outdueled the New York Mets, 6-0, that day to punch their ticket to the World Series.

4. Only five home runs have ever been hit completely out of Dodger Stadium. Two were hit by Willie Stargell of the Pittsburgh Pirates. In 1969, he crushed an offering by Alan Foster 507 feet (155 meters), denting a bus in the parking lot.

5. "Fernandomania" started in 1981, when Fernando Valenzuela blasted off, completing and winning each of his first eight starts. In 1980, he pitched 17.2 innings in relief at season's end, allowing just two runs, both of

which came in his first appearance. Lasorda decided not to start him in a one-game playoff against Houston for the NL West title and the Dodgers lost.

6. L.A. leveraged Valenzuela to tap into an ever-growing Hispanic market in the so-called Basin. He pitched a no-hitter in 1990 and Oakland's Dave Stewart copied his no-no on the same day, an MLB first.

7. Don Newcombe, from New Jersey, became the first African-American to star as a pitcher. In 1949 (two years after Jackie), he won the Rookie of the Year Award with Brooklyn and in 1956 he went 27-7 and won the NL MVP and Cy Young awards.

8. Yet Newcombe was a washout in the World Series. He stumbled to a 0-4 record in five starts, with an 8.59 ERA. In the decisive 1951 playoff game, he was yanked for Ralph Branca, who then yielded "the Shot Heard 'Round the World" homer by the Giants' Bobby Thomson.

9. Brooklyn's Burleigh Grimes was the last pitcher allowed to continue using the spitter after the pitch was banned. He changed teams eight times after leaving Brooklyn in 1926, came back to manage in 1937, and even suggested his replacement, Leo Durocher (instead of the more popular Babe Ruth).

10. Duke Snider went missing in his first World Series with Brooklyn in 1949, scratching out only three hits in 21 tries, with no RBI and eight strikeouts. However, in his next four Series, he hammered 10 homers, including four in the 1955 Classic to bury the Yankees.

CHAPTER 7:

DRAFT DAY

QUIZ TIME!

1. Up to 2018, of the 68 first-round draft picks by the Dodgers, how many have been pitchers?

    a. 24

    b. 29

    c. 37

    d. 45

2. Overall, five of the Dodgers' first-round picks have made it to the top by winning a World Series with L.A. Which of the following has NOT?

    a. Steve Howe

    b. Bob Welch

    c. Franklin Stubbs

    d. Tom Niedenfuer

3. Which state has provided the most first-round draft picks to L.A. over the years?

a. California

b. Nevada

c. Tennessee

d. Texas

4. Which first-round pick did the Dodgers fail to sign and also receive no compensation pick for?

a. Dave Anderson (1981)

b. Luke Hochevar (2005)

c. Rick Sutcliffe (1974)

d. Mike Scioscia (1976)

5. Shortstop Jesmuel Valentin was L.A.'s first-round pick in 2012. What school did he come from?

a. Conway High School (SC)

b. Stanford University (CA)

c. Puerto Rico Baseball Academy and High School

d. Vanderbilt University (TN)

6. As of 2020, how many of the Dodgers' 68 first-round picks have not made it to the major league level (not including the three still in the minor league system)?

a. 20

b. 25

c. 32

d. 39

7. Bobby Valentine was one of the most hyped picks in the 1968 draft, yet he spent a year in the minors and only three with L.A. before being traded. What was one move he made later as Mets manager that attracted attention?

a. He bought popcorn and ate it in the dugout.

b. He orchestrated a triple steal to win a game.

c. He was ejected from three consecutive games for arguing.

d. He wore a fake mustache in the dugout.

8. L.A.'s first pick in the 1985 draft was Chris Gwynn, younger brother of San Diego Padre star and Hall-of-Famer Tony. Did Chris ever match his older brother's production?

   a. Yes

   b. No

9. The Dodgers have never owned the first overall pick and have only had a top-five pick three times in their history. Who was their highest pick ever, the second overall, in 1993?

   a. Darren Dreifort

   b. Torii Hunter

   c. Trot Nixon

   d. Alex Rodriguez

10. Bob Welch came to the Dodgers in the 1977 amateur draft. He compiled a 115-86 record, a glowing 3.14 ERA, and four postseason appearances. With which team did he find more success after L.A.?

    a. The Arizona Diamondbacks

    b. The Oakland A's

    c. The San Francisco Giants

    d. The Seattle Mariners

11. Some call Clayton Kershaw the best Dodgers draft choice ever. He was the seventh overall pick in 2006 and pitched well at the Rookie, Single-A, and Double-A levels. How old was he when got the big-league call?

    a. 18
    b. 20
    c. 23
    d. 25

12. Steve Sax wasn't a great hitter or even a good fielder, but as the ninth-round pick in the 1978 draft, he became the leadoff man and part of the 1988 championship team. How many balls did he boot in his second full season in the majors?

    a. 12
    b. 20
    c. 30
    d. 42

13. An incredible athlete, Matt Kemp still slid to the sixth round in 2003. He's known as a "five-tool" player. Which skill is NOT included in this set?

    a. bunting
    b. fielding
    c. hitting
    d. running

14. Ron Cey was picked by L.A. in the third round of the 1968 draft. He turned out to be a prodigious slugger. How

many years did it take him to be the all-time Dodgers HR leader?

a. 11
b. 14
c. 17
d. 20

15. Cey had played 12 seasons for the L.A. when he finally won the World Series and the MVP in 1981. In how many previous World Series had he and his team come up empty?

a. 1
b. 2
c. 3
d. 5

16. First baseman Eric Karros was snapped up by the Dodgers as the sixth-round pick in 1988. What university did he come out of?

a. Pepperdine University
b. UCLA
c. USC
d. UNLV

17. 1968 was a disastrous year for the Dodgers on the field but their draft was a doozy: They picked up several players integral to their '70s success. Which of these players was NOT drafted in '68?

a. Bill Buckner

b. Steve Garvey

c. Davey Lopes

d. Pete Rose

18. One of the best draft picks in L.A. franchise history, Davey Lopes had a better stolen base percentage (83%) than Rickey Henderson, Lou Brock and Ty Cobb.

    a. True

    b. False

19. Catcher Mike Piazza might be the biggest draft-day steal of all time. In what 1988 round was he finally chosen by L.A.?

    a. The 44th

    b. The 51st

    c. The 62nd

    d. The 74th

20. Not only was he a draft-day gem, but Piazza is widely regarded as the best hitting catcher ever. What were his average BA and number of homers per year as a Dodger?

    a. .290+ & 30

    b. .300+ & 33.5

    c. .310+ & 36

    d. .325+ & 38

QUIZ ANSWERS

1. C — 36

2. D — Tom Niedenfuer

3. C — Tennessee

4. B — Luke Hochevar (2005)

5. C — Puerto Rico Baseball Academy and High School

6. C — 32

7. D — He wore a fake mustache in the dugout.

8. B — No

9. A — Darren Dreifort

10. B — The Oakland A's

11. B — 20

12. C — 30

13. A — Bunting is included in hitting.

14. B — 14

15. C — 3

16. B — UCLA

17. D — Pete Rose

18. A — True

19. C — The 62nd

20. B — .300+ / 33.5

DID YOU KNOW?

1. Originally picked in the 17th round of the 1979 draft, Orel Hershiser had a 1988 season and postseason that continues to inspire awe: most wins in the NL (23), most shutouts (8), most innings pitched (267), a Cy Young and a Gold Glove Award. The postseason? He won the NLCS and World Series MVP awards.

2. Mr. Clean, Mr. Popular, you name it — Steve Garvey was snagged by L.A. in the first round of the 1968 secondary draft and he earned his keep. A ten-time All-Star, a four-time Gold Glove winner and a 1981 World Series champ, Steve also played in 1,207 straight games — an NL record.

3. Some 55 years after its first amateur draft, MLB held its shortest draft event ever in 2020 — only five precious rounds — due to the global coronavirus pandemic.

4. Pitcher Walker Buehler was drafted by the Dodgers as the 24th overall pick in the 2015 draft. He was previously drafted in 2012 by the Pirates, but he stayed in school, honoring his commitment to Vanderbilt University.

5. On the other hand, Cody Bellinger made a verbal commitment to play baseball for the University of Oregon. But when he was drafted by L.A. in the fourth round of the 2013 draft, he took the $700K signing bonus. Cody's dad, Clay, had played for the Angels and Yanks.

6. In the 1993 draft, the debate was whether Seattle would pick Alex "A-Rod" Rodriguez or Darren Dreifort, who wound up being drafted by L.A. "I told them (the M's) not to draft me. I told them I wanted to play for the Dodgers, and I wanted to play in the National League so that I could get home a couple times a year," A-Rod recalled.

7. In the first-ever MLB draft in 1965, the Dodgers picked Bakersfield shortstop John Wyatt. "I knew I was probably going to get drafted but didn't realize I was going to get drafted the number one guy by the Dodgers," Wyatt reflected. He never made it in the majors.

8. Five number one picks of other clubs have found their way to L.A.: Rick Monday (1965/A's), Darryl Strawberry (1980/Mets), Tim Belcher (1983/Twins), Adrián González (2000/Marlins) and David Price (2007/Rays).

9. L.A. had its sights on Chase Utley in high school, drafting him in the second round in 1997. But Chase took a trip with his buddies before signing, liked the atmosphere, and decided he wanted to go to UCLA. He was eventually drafted by Philadelphia in the first round of the 2000 draft after three years with the Bruins.

10. Chad Billingsley, selected 24th by the Dodgers in 2003, pitched for the Ogden Raptors, the Vero Beach Dodgers, the Jacksonville Suns and the Las Vegas 51s before getting the nod from L.A. In his first MLB start, he was hit by a pitch and knocked in two runs in a win over the Padres.

CHAPTER 8:

PITCHER & CATCHER TIDBITS

QUIZ TIME!

1. Charles Arthur "Dazzy" Vance pitched in the minors for 10 years before he even got a crack with Brooklyn. Apparently, his arm was sore and one day a minor accident made him seek surgery. What happened?

    a. He banged his elbow trying to dodge a trolley car.
    b. He banged his elbow on a poker table.
    c. He was involved in fisticuffs over a poker bet.
    d. He injured his arm when he fell from a barstool.

2. It was said that Dazzy baffled many batters because the uniform sleeve on his pitching arm was "a flapping thing of shreds and tatters." As a result, a rule was passed preventing pitchers from wearing fluttery sleeves or white wristbands.

    a. True
    b. False

3. Vance never won a pennant with the Dodgers, but he was traded back to St. Louis in time to help them win one in 1934. What was the nickname of the group of Cards' players, including Dizzy and Paul Dean?

   a. The Gashouse Gang
   b. The Card House Gang
   c. The Dizzy Dazzyers
   d. The Lighthouse Family

4. Elwin Charles "Preacher" Roe, born in Ash Flat, Arkansas, was an ace Dodgers pitcher from 1948 to 1954. How did he get his nickname?

   a. He used to preach to his friends on the art and craft of baseball.
   b. His father and grandfather were both preachers.
   c. When an uncle asked his name at age three, he said "preacher" due to one who gave him horse-and-buggy rides.
   d. At age three, he used to "preach" to the horses on his father's farm.

5. Roe was still pitching in the majors at age 38 and was the third oldest player in the NL in 1954, his last season. To what did he attribute his long career?

   a. "Clean livin' and the spitball."
   b. "Lots of sleep and a clean ball to spit on."
   c. "Stay out of the bars, and keep the runners off the bags."
   d. "Listen to the coach, and then do what you want on the mound."

6. Ralph Branca pitched for the Dodgers on Opening Day in 1947, which was also Jackie Robinson's debut. What did Branca do then that others did not?

   a. He ran ten sprints before the game began.
   b. He sang the National Anthem at the top of his voice.
   c. He knelt during the National Anthem.
   d. He lined up willingly on the field alongside Robinson.

7. Branca remains the notorious Dodgers pitcher who gave up the walk-off homer, called "The Shot Heard 'Round the World," to the Giants' Bobby Thompson in a 1951 playoff. Bobby had already homered off Ralph in Game 1. Why was Branca even in the game?

   a. Carl Erskine, also warming up, suddenly felt faint and had to sit down.
   b. Carl Erskine, also warming up, had just bounced several balls in the bullpen dirt.
   c. Manager Charlie Dressen considered Thompson's Game 1 homer "lucky."
   d. Manager Charlie Dressen believed in second chances for players he liked.

8. Dodgers pitcher Don Sutton was born into a poor sharecropper's family in rural Alabama. What was he voted for by his high school classmates in 1963?

   a. Best All-Around Athlete
   b. Class Clown
   c. Class President
   d. Most Likely To Succeed

9. L.A. pitching sensation Don Drysdale was born in nearby Van Nuys. Who was one of his equally famous classmates in high school?

   a. Arnold Schwarzenegger
   b. Paul Newman
   c. Ronald Reagan
   d. Robert Redford

10. In 1968, Drysdale set an MLB record with six consecutive complete-game shutouts and 58.2 consecutive scoreless innings. Which L.A. hurler broke the latter record but not the former 20 years later?

    a. Rick Honeycutt
    b. Jerry Reuss
    c. Orel Hershiser
    d. Fernando Valenzuela

11. Sandy Koufax starred on the mound for the Dodgers despite his relatively short career. What was he the first MLB pitcher to do?

    a. Pitch consecutive perfect games
    b. Pitch four no-hitters
    c. Pitch three complete games in consecutive World Series
    d. Pitch two complete games on one day's rest

12. Koufax also won the NL Triple Crown for pitchers in 1963, 1965, and 1966. Which of the following categories is NOT included in the Triple Crown?

a. ERA
b. Strikeouts
c. Walks
d. Wins

13. Roy "Campy" Campanella played in the Negro League and in Mexico before being considered one of the greatest catchers in history with Brooklyn from 1948 to 1957. How did his career abruptly end?

   a. He was paralyzed in a car accident.
   b. He was badly injured in a home-plate collision.
   c. He was badly hurt when beaned by a pitch.
   d. He decided to stop playing because of a chronic knee injury.

14. Claude Osteen was acquired by the Dodgers from the Washington Senators and developed into a top starter with a 3.00 ERA. What phrase was used to describe Osteen in the 1965 Series win over the Twins?

   a. A flamethrower
   b. A playboy
   c. A "whale" of a pitcher
   d. A workhorse

15. Known as one of the best defensive catchers of the '60s, John Roseboro was the L.A. starter in four World Series, of which they won three. What violent incident was he was involved in on the field?

   a. He single-handedly fought off five Giants players simultaneously.

b. The Giants' Juan Marichal struck him in the head with a bat.

c. He was attacked by plate umpire Shag Crawford after arguing strikes.

d. The Giants' Juan Marichal struck him in the head with a ball.

16. Catcher Steve Yeager was a cousin of test pilot Chuck Yeager and married local rock star Gloria Giaone in 1976. Who was the best man at the grand event?

a. Actor Sly Stallone

b. L.A. Mayor Tom Bradley

c. President Gerald Ford

d. Actor Jack Nicholson

17. Yeager helped the Dodgers get to the Series in 1974, 1977, 1978 and 1981. Even though he was the backup to Mike Scioscia at the time, he ended up sharing the 1981 World Series MVP award with two other Dodgers for his timely hitting. Who did NOT share the award with Yeager?

a. Ron Cey

b. Pedro Guerrero

c. Bill Russell

18. Mike Piazza put up fabulous offensive numbers playing for the Dodgers and Mets. Besides being the former owner of an Italian soccer team, what other odd job does he do?

a. Black Label Society's lead drummer

b. Italy national baseball team manager

c. New York City pizzeria owner

d. New York City Uber driver

19. Piazza surely ranks as one of the best hitting catchers of all time. Who does NOT join him on the list of players with more than 400 career homers, an average over .300 and never striking out more than 100 times in a season?

a. Hank Aaron

b. Babe Ruth

c. Chipper Jones

d. Kenny Landreaux

20. Former Dodgers VP Al Campanis called Mike Scioscia the best plate-blocking catcher he'd ever seen. One 1986 collision Scioscia recalls was against a steamrolling Chili Davis of the Giants. What did Mike say about the incident?

a. "He was out. We were both out."

b. "I don't remember a thing, but they told me I made a nice tag."

c. "I never wanted to dine on chili again after that."

d. "All that matters is we won the game."

QUIZ ANSWERS

1. B — He banged his arm on a poker table.

2. A — True

3. A — The Gashouse Gang

4. C — When an uncle asked his name at age three, he said "preacher" due to one who gave him horse-and-buggy rides.

5. A — "Clean livin' and the spitball."

6. D — He lined up willingly on the field alongside Robinson.

7. B — Carl Erskine, also warming up, had just bounced several balls in the bullpen dirt. /

8. D — Most Likely To Succeed

9. D — Robert Redford

10. C — Orel Hershiser

11. B — Pitch four no-hitters

12. C — Walks

13. A — He was paralyzed in a car accident.

14. D — A workhorse

15. B — The Giants' Juan Marichal struck him in the head with a bat.

16. B — L.A. Mayor Tom Bradley

17. C — Bill Russell

18. B — Italy national baseball team manager

19. D — Kenny Landreaux

20. A — "He was out. We were both out."

DID YOU KNOW?

1. Mike Scioscia amazingly used the same catcher's mitt for most of his 12-year career. He caught two no-hitters: one by Fernando Valenzuela in 1990 and the other by Kevin Gross in 1992. Mike was on the receiving end of 136 shutouts, fourth best of ML catchers in history.

2. Shortstop Alfredo Griffin, one of Scioscia's teammates on the 1988 World Series-winning team, was invited by Mike to join him on the coaching staff of the L.A. Angels from 2000 to 2018.

3. On June 6, 2006, L.A. catcher Russell Martin and his mate on the mound, Eric Gagné, made MLB history. They became the first French-Canadian battery in the big leagues.

4. In May 2007, Martin stole a base to break the single-season Dodgers stolen base record of 12 for catchers, set by John Roseboro, and finished with 21 that season. Russell went on to become the first Canadian-born catcher to start the All-Star Game that same year.

5. The L.A. bridge to South Korea was opened by pitcher Hyun-jin Ryu, the first pitcher to take advantage of the "posting" or transfer system between the U.S. and that country. He also turned out to be the first Korean pitcher to start a World Series game in 2013.

6. In fact, Chan Ho Park came from South Korea before Ryu. At one point, he passed Hideo Nomo for the most wins by any Asia-born pitcher. Alas, he was also the only hurler in MLB history to give up two grand slam home runs in the same inning — to the same player, no less (the Cards' Fernando Tatís in 1999).

7. Besides being involved in an on-field brawl against the Angels when Tim Belcher apparently tagged him too hard on a bunt play, Park was also the pitcher who gave up the record-breaking 71st and 72nd home runs by the Giants' Barry Bonds in 2001.

8. Japanese pitcher Hideo Nomo wasn't initially selected to play pro ball because of control issues. He joined an industrial league team in Osaka in 1988 and slept with a tennis ball taped between his fingers to improve his forkball grip.

9. When Nomo finally made it with the Dodgers, he was followed by throngs of Japanese reporters and his games were broadcast live to Japan despite the time difference. He is the only pitcher to record a no-hitter at Denver's Coors Field, a hitter's park where balls carry in the thin air and there's no foul territory.

10. Yasmani Grandal, a Cuban-American, became the third catcher in history to have three homers in a five-hit game. He also tied Mike Piazza and Roy Campanella with his three dingers in a single game and was rewarded with a $5.5 million contract in 2017 from the Dodgers.

CHAPTER 9:

ODDS & ENDS

QUIZ TIME!

1. In 2007, the Dodgers decided to convert their formerly cheap right field seats into a slightly more expensive "All-You-Can-Eat Pavilion." Which of the following is NOT available there for "free"?

   a. Beer
   b. Dodger Dogs
   c. Nachos
   d. Soft drinks

2. When the Dodgers tested the "all-you-can-eat concept" during the 2006 season, what was the fan response?

   a. Many fans complained of stomachaches
   b. Fans were overwhelmingly positive
   c. Most fans wanted spicier food
   d. Many fans refused to leave after the game

3. Until 1955, the Brooklyn Dodgers had appeared in seven World Series, including five against their cross-city rivals,

the New York Yankees, and lost every time. What was the team called at the time?

a. Baseball's bridesmaids
b. Baseball's born losers
c. Baseball's buffoons
d. The best team that never won

4. When the Brooklyn team started Jackie Robinson in their season opener in 1947, which team opposed them?

a. The Atlanta Braves
b. The Boston Americans
c. The Boston Braves
d. The St. Louis Browns

5. The fact that Jackie Robinson would be the first African-American player to break the MLB "color line" on that fine day was not even the biggest story in Brooklyn. What was?

a. The dramatic increase in train fares at Penn Station
b. The vast corruption scandal in the NYPD
c. Manager Leo Durocher's season-long suspension after a spat with GM Larry MacPhail
d. The smallpox scare in N.Y. City

6. On May 7, 1959, L.A. paid tribute to the former Dodgers catcher, Roy Campanella, who had been paralyzed in a 1958 auto accident. Most of those in attendance had never seen him play due to the team's recent move west. What was the record-breaking attendance for that exhibition game?

a. 75,157

b. 86,268

c. 93,103

d. 99,198

7. Rick Monday became an L.A. fan favorite before he ever wore a Dodgers jersey. What did he do while still with the Cubs in 1976 to make this happen?

   a. He said repeatedly that L.A. was a better place to play than Chicago.

   b. He joined fans in the first row of outfield seats for a beer during the 7th-inning stretch.

   c. He rescued a stray cat from aggressive security guards.

   d. He rescued an American flag about to be burned in the outfield by protestors.

8. When Walter O'Malley considered moving the Dodgers west in 1958, the owner of the Hollywood Stars in L.A. was also considering a stadium for Chavez Ravine, including a golf course, swimming pool, and parking for 50,000 cars.

   a. True

   b. False

9. When Chavez Ravine and the surrounding hills were finally reshaped for the new Dodger Stadium, what was the fate of an elementary school standing in the way?

   a. It was simply buried and now lies under the parking lot behind third base.

b. It was carefully moved using cranes and helicopters.

c. It was torn down.

d. It was auctioned off piece by piece.

10. Ex-Dodgers owner Frank McCourt sold the franchise in 2012 for $2.15 billion. What stake does he still have in the parking lots around the stadium?

a. 10%

b. 25%

c. 50%

d. 65%

11. When the Dodgers aren't playing during the day, what can you do for free in the upper deck of the stadium?

a. Enter the top gate behind home plate with your lunch, without being asked to leave.

b. Participate in a ping pong tournament held there.

c. Take batting practice with some substitute Dodgers.

d. Tour the upper deck and the locker rooms accompanied by a bilingual guide.

12. Mike Brito, a Dodgers scout born in Cuba, was a feature for years at Dodger Stadium in his Panama hat with his radar gun. Which famed Latin players did he uncover?

a. Vinny Castilla and Jorge Orta

b. Beto Ávila and Aurelio Rodríguez

c. Fernando Valenzuela and Yasiel Puig

d. José Calderón and Robin Lopez

13. While owner Walter O'Malley waited for Dodger Stadium to develop, he took the team to the colossal L.A. Coliseum.

Some fans sat 700 feet from home plate but nearly 8 million of them poured in during four years there. True or False?

   a. True

   b. False

14. O'Malley also formed a partnership with Union 76, an oil company, to bring in extra revenue. What did the Dodgers allow Union to do in return?

   a. Construct a gas refinery just beyond one parking lot.

   b. Plant a gas station right in the middle of the parking lot.

   c. Plant a row of gorgeous trees beyond the outfield wall.

   d. Offer seeds to all youth players to protect the environment.

15. Strangely enough, heavy rain almost caused the cancellation of Opening Day in 1962 at the brand-new Dodger Stadium. What was one suggestion a Hollywood director made for getting the field ready?

   a. Create numerous showbiz effects to distract the fans.

   b. Hire Hollywood actresses to make the fans forget the game.

   c. Paint the field green to make it look fresh and ready.

   d. Paint the field blue to force the fans to remember the team color.

16. Dodger Stadium quickly gained a reputation as a pitcher's park, mainly due to cool Pacific breezes blowing in. Which great hitter batted .377 in 79 games at Chavez Ravine?

a. Roberto Clemente

b. Willie Mays

c. Reggie Smith

d. Mike Schmidt

17. Another fixture at Dodger Stadium in the 1970s was long-time peanut vendor Roger Owens. He freaked the fans with his accurate and acrobatic tosses of peanut bags. What was he invited to do because of his talent?

a. Endorse all products from peanut butter giant Jiffy

b. Represent the U.S. in the International Snack Olympics

c. Toss peanut bags at President Jimmy Carter's inaugural party

d. Become the official peanut vendor of the MLB

18. By far the most popular and best-tasting treat in the park is the long, skinny Dodger Dog. In the 1980s, which player in full uniform actually waited in line for one?

a. Yu Darvish

b. Jay Johnstone

c. Delino DeShields

d. Darryl Strawberry

19. "Fernandomania" brought fans back to the park after a dry spell in the 1970s. Then the Dodgers passed 3 million fans around the Millennium. Which team that drew 4,483,350 in 1993 does L.A. hope to match?

a. The Atlanta Braves

b. The Colorado Rockies

c. The New York Yankees

d. The Kansas City Royals

20. After the Dodgers' sale by Frank McCourt, a deep-pocketed group headed by Guggenheim Partners had ambitious plans for renovating the stadium. Who was NOT included in this group?

a. Basketball legend Magic Johnson

b. Hollywood honcho Peter Guber

c. Baseball exec Stan Kasten

d. Kung Fu hero Jackie Chan

QUIZ ANSWERS

1. A — Beer

2. B — Fans were overwhelmingly positive

3. A — Baseball's bridesmaids

4. C — The Boston Braves

5. C — Manager Leo Durocher's season-long suspension after a spat with the GM, Larry MacPhail

6. C — 93,103

7. D — He rescued an American flag about to be burned in the outfield by protestors.

8. B — False / The stadium would have parking for 30,000 cars.

9. A — It was simply buried, and now lies under the parking lot behind third base.

10. C — 50%

11. A — Enter the top gate behind home plate with your lunch, without being asked to leave.

12. C — Fernando Valenzuela and Yasiel Puig

13. A — True

14. B — Plant a gas station right in the middle of a parking lot.

15. C — Paint the field green to make it look fresh and ready.

16. A — Roberto Clemente

17. C — Toss peanut bags at President Jimmy Carter's inaugural party

18. B — Jay Johnstone

19. B — The Colorado Rockies

20. D — Kung Fu hero Jackie Chan

DID YOU KNOW?

1. Dave Roberts, the current Dodgers manager, is the son of a Japanese mother and African-American father. In 2017, he became the first manager of Asian heritage to lead a team to the World Series.

2. When Roberts played for the Caguas Criollos in Puerto Rico on his way to the majors, he teamed up with Alex Cora and Joey Cora, the team's GM. Practically 20 years later, Dave faced off against Alex, the manager of the Boston Red Sox, in the 2018 Series.

3. At Brooklyn's Ebbets Field in 1931, there was a prominent sign that read, "Hit Sign, Win Suit. Abe Stark." Any Dodgers player who dinged the centerfield plaque won a suit from local clothier Stark. An employee said that Stark was altering suits for more players than other customers.

4. On the other hand, when somebody pointed out that rightfielder Carl Furillo had snagged many long flies, saving Stark a number of suits, the tailor generously promised Furillo a free set of threads. Finally, according to teammate Duke Snider, all Carl ever received was a pair of slacks.

5. Floyd Caves "Babe" Herman, born in Buffalo, bruised the ball for Brooklyn while setting the following franchise records in 1930: .393 BA, .678 slugging percentage, 241 hits and 416 total bases. In his career, this particular Babe hit for the cycle on a record three different occasions.

6. The Dodgers games in New York were broadcast by Channel 9, which was cable TV before cable. It showed old movies, bygone police shows and all the N.Y. sports teams — for free.

7. Chuck Essegian will forever be a Dodgers hero for his two pinch-hit homers in the 1959 World Series triumph over the Chicago White Sox. Boston's Bernie Carbo later equaled the mark with two pinch home runs in the 1975 Series. The Dodgers won theirs, while the BoSox did not.

8. Though Walter Alston managed the Dodgers longer, Tommy Lasorda won two NL pennants in his first two years at the helm, 1977 and 1978. When MLB established the "Manager of the Year" award in 1983, Lasorda won the first in the NL. In his first year of eligibility after stepping down in 1996, Tommy entered the Hall of Fame as a manager in 1997. Finally, his number (2) was retired by the Dodgers.

9. In 1977, the Dodgers were the first team ever with four players who hit 30 or more round-trippers in a season. Steve Garvey was the first to the mark, followed by Reggie Smith and then Ron Cey. Finally, Dusty Baker cleared the fences on the last day of the season versus the Astros' J.R. Richard.

10. Some of us may have mulled over the same idea, but who was the umpire who was actually attacked by a fan at Ebbets Field in 1940? His name was George Magerkurth, and the assailant apparently a parole violator. The Dodgers in the meantime had just lost to the Reds, 4-3.

CHAPTER 10:

WHO'S ON FIRST?

QUIZ TIME!

1. Jake Daubert was one of the first great first basemen in a long Dodgers line (at that time the Brooklyn Superbas). In his career from 1910 to 1924, what was his lowest fielding percentage?

    a. .972
    b. .980
    c. .989
    d. .995

2. In 1895, the lack of child labor laws allowed Jake to go to work at age 11 with his father and two brothers. What did he do before baseball?

    a. He delivered newspapers on a bicycle.
    b. He worked in the local coal mines.
    c. He worked in a local bat-making factory.
    d. He helped in his father's hardware store.

3. On August 15, 1914, Daubert tied a major league record held by Cy Seymour. What was the mark?

    a. He laid down four sacrifice bunts in a single game.

    b. He was the winning pitcher and also hit three homers.

    c. He stole every base on the way to scoring the game-winning run.

    d. He stole the opponents' signs and then hit for the cycle.

4. Which of the following was NOT one of the reasons Daubert's (and everyone else's) 1918 MLB season was cut short?

    a. An umpires' strike

    b. The Spanish flu epidemic

    c. World War I

5. Before moving to Brooklyn, Jack Fournier presented his 1912 Chicago manager with a dilemma: what to do with his hot hitting and sub-par fielding? By the way, what was that manager's name?

    a. Frank Chance

    b. Red Dooin

    c. Connie Mack

    d. Pants Rowland

6. At the time Fournier played, the first baseman's position was considered one of the key fielding positions. Why?

    a. The first baseman covered more ground then as the second baseman stood on the bag,

b. The first baseman had to constantly play the bunt.

c. The first baseman was not allowed to wear a large glove yet.

d. The first baseman was closer to the stands and had to deal with more hecklers.

7. Adelphia "Del" Louis Bissonette, born in Winthrop, Maine, brought his booming bat to the Brooklyn Robins in 1928. In 1930, he became the first MLB player to achieve a rare hitting feat. What was it?

a. He hit for the cycle and stole four bases.

b. He fouled off ten straight pitches before connecting on a grand slam.

c. He hit a bases-loaded triple and a bases-loaded homer in the same game.

d. He hit safely in ten consecutive at-bats.

8. Dolph Camilli was the Dodgers' first baseman when they won the 1941 pennant for the first time in 20 years. Because of his free-swinging style, he tied the previous season strikeout mark of 94. With whom?

a. Joe DiMaggio

b. Doc Cramer

c. Ted Williams

d. Hack Wilson

9. Camilli became an All-Star and the Dodgers' team captain, but the strikeouts continued to pile up. He soon broke the NL career record held by Rabbit Maranville. What was Maranville's tally?

a. 656

b. 726

c. 756

d. 834

10. When Dolph Camilli was traded to the New York Giants in 1943, what did he decide to do?

    a. He decided to retire to focus more on fishing and eating.

    b. He took a sabbatical year to study abroad.

    c. He refused to report to the Dodgers' hated rivals.

    d. He wept openly in public on several occasions.

11. Gil Hodges, who played for both Brooklyn and L.A., was considered one of the best defensive first basemen of the 1950s. How many assists and double plays did he have when his 18-year career ended?

    a. 987 & 1,244

    b. 1,024 & 1,389

    c. 1,155 & 1,510

    d. 1,281 & 1,614

12. Hodges went on to manage the Miracle (N.Y.) Mets in 1969 in one of the greatest upsets in World Series history. Who were the opponents?

    a. The Baltimore Orioles

    b. The Boston Red Sox

    c. The New York Yankees

    d. The Minnesota Twins

13. On a beautiful 1950 day at the ballpark, Hodges became only the second player since 1900 to hit four homers in the same game without extra innings. Who was the other player who did it?

    a. Enos Slaughter

    b. Lou Gehrig

    c. Mel Ott

    d. Johnny Mize

14. When Hodges went hitless at the end of the 1952 season and then again in all seven games of the World Series versus the Yankees, what did a Brooklyn priest tell his flock?

    a. "Every man needs to help the next. But who can help dear Hodges?"

    b. "Keep the faith, and love thy neighbor—but never the Yankees."

    c. "Thou shalt not steal, but pray for the Dodgers to steal a game against the Yankees."

    d. "Keep the commandments and say a prayer for Gil Hodges."

15. First baseman Wes Parker was an integral part of L.A.'s 1965 and 1966 World Series teams. Which team did he play for in Japan later in his career?

    a. The Hiroshima Toyo Carp

    b. The Kintetsu Buffaloes

    c. The Nankai Hawks

    d. The Yakult Swallows

16. Parker's slick fielding at first earned him a berth on the MLB all-time Gold Glove Team. However, he did not and will never be a Hall of Fame member. Why not?

    a. He played only nine seasons, while 10 are required for the Hall.

    b. He left to play in Japan before his L.A. contract had fully expired.

    c. He was caught evading taxes owed to the Feds and was thus disciplined.

    d. His fielding stats were out of this world but his hitting stats were mundane.

17. After winning six Gold Glove Awards at first, Wes Parker pursued some other alternative jobs. Which of the following is NOT one he tried?

    a. He became a baseball broadcaster for NBC and the USA Network.

    b. He became a successful interpreter for the Japanese government.

    c. He served as a "Voice of Faith" for the ministry of TV preacher Gene Scott.

    d. He starred in one episode of "The Brady Bunch."

18. Steve Garvey, "Mr. Clean," was the Dodgers first baseman and resident slugger from 1973 to 1982. Although Cal Ripken has the MLB mark, Garvey holds the record for most consecutive games played in the NL. How many?

    a. 1,001

    b. 1,076

c. 1,207

d. 1,340

19. After his parents had relocated from Long Island to Tampa, Florida, the young Garvey got close to several MLB teams in spring training, including the Brooklyn Dodgers, Detroit Tigers and New York Yankees. What did he do for them?

   a. He was a batboy.

   b. He was a water boy.

   c. He was a "youth security guard."

   d. He shined the players' shoes.

20. Garvey was a cornerstone of one of the most durable MLB infields, which managed to stay together for eight and a half years in the 1970s. Who was NOT a member of the gang?

   a. Ron Cey

   b. Davey Lopes

   c. Bill Russell

   d. Ted Sizemore

QUIZ ANSWERS

1. C — .989

2. B — He worked in the local coal mines.

3. A — He laid down four sacrifice bunts in a single game.

4. A — An umpires' strike

5. D — Pants Rowland

6. B — The first baseman had to constantly play the bunt.

7. C — He hit a bases-loaded triple and a bases-loaded homer in the same game.

8. D — Hack Wilson

9. C — 756

10. C — He refused to report to the Dodgers' hated rivals.

11. D — 1,281 / 1,614

12. A — The Baltimore Orioles

13. B — Lou Gehrig

14. D — "Keep the commandments and say a prayer for Gil Hodges."

15. C — The Nankai Hawks

16. A — He played only nine seasons, while 10 are required for the Hall.

17. B — He became a successful interpreter for the Japanese government.

18. C — 1,207

19. A — He was a batboy.

20. D — Ted Sizemore

DID YOU KNOW?

1. Steve Garvey is one of only two MLB players to go to the All-Star Game as a result of a write-in vote. It happened in 1974, the year he won the NL MVP Award. It was also the first time he had more than 200 hits in a season, a feat he repeated five more times.

2. When free agent Garvey was signed away from the Dodgers in 1982 by San Diego general manager Jack McKeon, that team increased its season ticket sales by 6,000. Meanwhile, Garvey's undying popularity in L.A. even led some Girl Scouts to picket Dodger Stadium.

3. Garvey had political aspirations after his career — his teammates even called him "Senator." But personal scandals ended that ambition. Steve still set up a blue marlin fishing event and a celeb skiing challenge, hosted a show called "Baseball's Greatest Games" and did some motivational speaking.

4. Franklin Stubbs came out of Virginia Tech, played for the Albuquerque Dukes in the Pacific Coast League, and finally helped the Dodgers win the 1988 Series. In 1987, Stubbs handled 885 total chances at first with only five errors for a .994 fielding percentage.

5. Eric Karros, out of Hackensack, NJ, won the 1992 NL Rookie of the Year Award. He also joined rarified Dodgers

company (namely Gil Hodges and Duke Snider) when he racked up 30 homers and 100 RBI in five different seasons.

6. Karros also lays claim to being the Dodgers' all-time leader in sacrifice flies with 74, the only Dodger to ever hit two homers in one inning, and the owner of the most home runs for a Dodgers player born in New Jersey (284).

7. James Loney played first base for the Dodgers but he blew the ball past hitters as a teen, playing for a Texas team in the "Reviving Baseball In Inner Cities" program. He sported a 12-1 record, 120 strikeouts, a 1.52 ERA, and a .500 BA as a senior in high school. In 2002, he was the Gatorade Player of the Year in Texas.

8. Loney received his big-league shot when Nomar Garciaparra was ruled out at first due to injury. In September 2006, he collected four hits and nine RBI in a game against the Rockies, tying a 56-year-old record set by Gil Hodges.

9. Adrián González was born into a baseball family. His dad was a member of the Mexican national team and his brother Edgar had his time in the big leagues as well. The two realized a dream when they played together for San Diego in 2008.

10. Cody Bellinger showed hints of his power by crushing five homers in his first 11 starts for L.A. and went on to have four multi-homer games in his first 45 (besting the previous MLB record held by Bob Horner who did it in 63 in 1978). Alas, he fell to eventual champ Aaron Judge in the 2017 Home Run Derby.

CHAPTER 11:

WHO'S GOT SECOND?

QUIZ TIME!

1. It was agreed that Jackie Robinson could really play second base. But, in fact, he broke into the big leagues at a different position. What was it?

   a. Centerfield
   b. First base
   c. Shortstop
   d. Pitcher

2. Jackie Robinson is the only player in MLB history to have his number (42) retired game-wide.

   a. True
   b. False

3. A true trailblazer and leader, Jackie Robinson was also one of The Boys of Summer who saw the Dodgers win six pennants in his 10 seasons. He was a first-ballot Hall-of-Famer but finished second in voting behind one player in 1962. Who?

a. Bob Feller

b. Kiki Kuyler

c. Phil Rizzuto

d. Red Ruffing

4. During the off-season, Robinson went on a vaudeville tour of the South where he answered pre-set questions about his life. Did he make more money on these tours than from his Dodgers' contract?

a. Yes

b. No

5. When Brooklyn baseball wasn't occupying his time, Robinson and businessman Dunbar McLaurin founded the Freedom National Bank in Harlem. Jackie was also the first chairman of the board. Who later served as the Chair?

a. U.S. President Lyndon Johnson

b. Robinson's brother, Mack

c. Robinson's wife, Rachel

d. Robinson's sister, Willa Mae

6. Davey Lopes had surprising power for a second baseman, but his burning speed and base-stealing ability made him a stalwart. What record does he hold for Dodgers second basemen?

a. Most switch-hit homers (45)

b. Five stolen base titles as a leadoff hitter

c. Six World Series wins

d. Seven Opening Day starts

7. Though Davey made his fame and fortune as a Dodger, he was born far from La-La Land. Where?

    a. Delaware
    b. Hawaii
    c. Montana
    d. Rhode Island

8. Lopes used his sheer speed and guile to steal a record number of bases. In 1975, he broke a 53-year-old record. What was it?

    a. 28 consecutive stolen bases without getting caught
    b. 38 consecutive stolen bases without getting caught
    c. 48 consecutive stolen bases without getting caught
    d. 18 consecutive stolen bases without having to slide

9. The versatile Jim Gilliam was a leadoff man and a second baseman. What did he allow Jackie Robinson to do?

    a. To go fishing more often on his days off
    b. To play third base which was easier on Robinson's bum knee
    c. To catch a ride to the park in Gilliam's new limo
    d. To platoon at second base

10. Gilliam was a footnote in the decisive 1955 Brooklyn win over the Yankees. He was moved to second, making way for speedy Cuban Sandy Amorós in left field. Then Amorós snagged Yogi Berra's drive to save Brooklyn. Who did Gilliam replace?

    a. Hank Bauer
    b. Gil Hodges

c. Pee Wee Reese

d. Don Zimmer

11. Junior Gilliam was reputedly an average fielder, but the Dodgers used him at every position except pitcher, catcher, and shortstop. What part of Jim's equipment is on display today in Cooperstown?

a. His batting glove

b. His fielding glove

c. His flip-down glasses

d. His unwashed cap

12. Before Brooklyn, Gilliam's manager in Baltimore saw he had trouble hitting curves from right-handers. He shouted, "Hey Junior, get over on the other side of the plate!" Switch-hitting helped Gilliam get to first more quickly. Who was the skipper?

a. Billy Cox

b. Clem Labine

c. George "Tubby" Scales

d. George "Shotgun" Shuba

13. When the Dodgers' legendary manager Walter Alston stepped aside in 1976, Tommy Lasorda got the call to replace him. What did he ask Gilliam to do?

a. Go to Blinkie's to pick up a dozen donuts

b. Join him as part of the Dodgers' coaching staff

c. Send his coaching résumé around to gauge other teams' interest

d. Think about a new career as a player agent

14. Steve Sax was called up from Double-A in 1981, in part rushing the departure of Davey Lopes. Sax had to overcome "a case of the yips" in 1983 and 1984. What was that?

    a. A condition similar to hiccups
    b. A sudden inability to follow the coach's instructions
    c. A sudden inability to swing the bat
    d. A sudden inability to throw the ball accurately

15. As a result of his 30 errors in 1983, many on routine throws to first, a name was coined for the condition: "Steve Sax Syndrome." What a similar malady called for pitchers?

    a. "Don Drysdale Disease"
    b. "Steve Blass Disease"
    c. "Steve Carlton Condition"
    d. "Tom Seaver Syndrome"

16. Sax's teammate, outfielder Pedro Guerrero, was forced to play third in 1983. His second thought was, "I hope they don't hit it to Sax." What was his first?

    a. "Help the Dodgers, Sax, and me—and not necessarily in that order!"
    b. "I hope they don't hit it at all."
    c. "I hope they don't hit it to me."
    d. "Why is fielding so important all of a sudden?"

17. Jeff Kent is the all-time leader in home runs for second basemen. He led the Dodgers in numerous categories in 2005. Which of the following was NOT his forte?

a. Batting average
b. On-base percentage
c. Slugging
d. Triples

18. While playing previously with the Giants, Kent suffered a broken wrist. He claimed he broke it while washing his car. What did the team finally determine?

    a. Kent had overextended himself playing too much ping pong.
    b. Kent had crashed his motorcycle while doing wheelies.
    c. Kent had suffered a bad fall while waterskiing.
    d. Kent had crashed his mountain bike while showing off for his kids.

19. Kent had an ongoing feud with another Giant, prompting one reporter to quip, "The one who lives longer will attend the other's funeral, just to make sure he's dead." Who was the other player?

    a. Barry Bonds
    b. Carl Everett
    c. Derek Bell
    d. José Vizcaíno

20. Despite a long productive career, what was Kent's last lament when he retired from the Dodgers in 2009 after 17 years in the majors?

    a. He lamented not passing Ryan Sandberg for most homers by a second baseman.

b. He said, "Being a Game 7 loser is the worst feeling that I've ever had as an athlete."
c. The fact that he had lied to Giants' management about his motorcycle.
d. The fact that he would have to live out his days in Austin, TX.

QUIZ ANSWERS

1. B — First base

2. A — True

3. A — Bob Feller

4. A — Yes

5. C — Robinson's wife, Rachel

6. D — Seven Opening Day starts

7. D — Rhode Island

8. B — 38 consecutive stolen bases without getting caught

9. B — To play third base which was easier on Robinson's bum knee

10. D — Don Zimmer

11. B — His fielding glove

12. C — George "Tubby" Scales

13. B — Join him as part of the Dodgers' coaching staff

14. D — A sudden inability to throw the ball accurately

15. B — "Steve Blass Disease"

16. C — "I hope they don't hit it to me!"

17. D — Triples

18. B — Kent had crashed his motorcycle while doing wheelies.

19. A — Barry Bonds

20. B — He said, "Being a Game 7 loser is the worst feeling that I've ever had as an athlete."

DID YOU KNOW?

1. The slim possibility of the Dodgers winning a virtual World Series in 2020 came crashing down when second baseman Gavin Lux was beaten online by the Rays' Blake Snell in the MLB The Show Players League quarterfinals.

2. At 37, Jeff Kent was the oldest Dodger ever to make it to the All-Star Game in 2005. He was passed two years after by Takashi Saito, who was 19 days older.

3. Enrique Hernández arrived in L.A. by way of Miami in 2014 and played seven different positions, mostly second base in 2019. The Puerto Rican is known for his sense of humor, including wearing a banana suit in the dugout while injured in 2015.

4. After batting reasonably well in 2017, Hernández roasted the ball in Game 5 of the NLCS with 3 homers, including a grand slam and 7 RBI (tying the postseason record for most runs batted in). The Dodgers made it to the World Series for the first time since 1988.

5. Jamey Carroll helped L.A. by covering for an injured Rafael Furcal at shortstop. In 2011, Jamey played second and got into the record books, tying for the fewest RBI (16) by any Dodger with 400 or more at-bats.

6. Mark Ellis signed with L.A. to play second. In 2012, he was hit by a hard Tyler Green slide, breaking up a double play. Ellis only went to the hospital the next day where doctors said he could have lost his leg due to the delay.

7. With the A's in 2006, Ellis broke Bret Boone's single-season AL fielding mark (.99685) for second baggers. Yet, he lost the Gold Glove to Mark Grudzielanek, who had a lower fielding average. That's because the Gold Glove is a result of a vote by MLB managers and coaches.

8. Mark Ellis was the model for one of the characters in the movie "Moneyball" about the A's analytical attempt to put together a competitive big-league team in a small market.

9. More famous for his stint with the Phillies, Chase Utley brought his aggressive base running to L.A. in 2015. In the NLCS, he broke up an inning-ending double play, breaking Ruben Tejada's leg in the process. The Dodgers won, but Utley was suspended (a decision eventually dropped).

10. Utley had a career-high six hits for the Dodgers on July 6, 2016. At the age of 37, he was the third oldest MLB player to do so. He was honored with the "Roy Campanella Award" for the year.

CHAPTER 12:

WHO'S AT THE HOT CORNER?

QUIZ TIME!

1. Pedro Guerrero could be called the best Dodgers third baseman ever, but he played more in the outfield. What did sabermetrics man Bill James say about Guerrero?

   a. "No need for sabermetrics analysis with Pedro"
   b. "He's the master of Dominican dingers"
   c. "The best hitter God has made in a long time"
   d. "Why can't we have eight Pedros and a pitcher?"

2. As a kid growing up in San Juan, Pedro supported his divorced mother by cutting cane, enjoyed playing drums in the evening and then tore the cover off the ball in a weekend league.

   a. True
   b. False

3. When Pedro finally broke into the big leagues in 1978, he pinch hit for his former minor league roomie (and future

nemesis) and singled for the first of his 1,618 hits. Who was the roomie?

   a. Burt Hooton

   b. Rudy Law

   c. Rick Sutcliffe

   d. Don Sutton

4. Adrián Beltré, another Dominican prodigy, garnered his highest MVP vote total as a Dodger. But his stretches with other teams were even better. For which of the following did he NOT play?

   a. Boston

   b. Cleveland

   c. Seattle

   d. Texas

5. Beltré hit a major league-leading 48 homers for L.A. in 2004. What was he the fifth major leaguer to ever do?

   a. Hit 100 homers for three different teams

   b. Play four different positions for three different teams

   c. Receive speeding tickets in three different MLB cities

   d. Lead the league in hits for three different teams

6. Upon his retirement in 2018, Adrián held several all-time records for third basemen. Which of these is one record he did NOT own?

   a. Hits

   b. Putouts

   c. RBI

   d. Runs scored

7. After Justin Turner arrived in 2004, he transformed himself into a top contact hitter and a deadly playoff bat (with a .310 playoff BA). What else has he become?

  a. An icon in the city of L.A.
  b. A much-in-demand Hollywood actor
  c. A Starbucks franchise owner
  d. A top salesman for beard-trimming kits

8. Turner attended California State University-Fullerton and was named to the all-tournament team in the 2003 College World Series. What was his college major?

  a. Biology
  b. Ceramics
  c. Kinesiology
  d. Nuclear Physics

9. When Justin turned free agent after playing with the Mets up to 2013, an L.A. bench coach saw him slugging at a Cal State-Fullerton alumni game. Who was the scout?

  a. Trey Hillman
  b. Don Mattingly
  c. Dixie Walker
  d. Tim Wallach

10. In the 2015 NLCS against his former team, the New York Mets, Turner starred with a .526 average. But L.A. was eliminated. How much was the one-year deal Justin that signed that offseason to avoid arbitration?

  a. $2.6 million

b. $3.9 million

c. $5.1 million

d. $6.5 million

11. The king of the hot corner in Los Angeles has long been considered Ron Cey, "The Penguin." Who adorned him with the cute nickname?

a. His father, Frank

b. His college coach, Chuck "Bobo" Brayton

c. His teammate, Davey Lopes

d. His minor league coach, Tommy Lasorda

12. Cey was born in Tacoma, Washington, and had the luck to play in front of his parents in Seattle's Kingdome at the 1979 All-Star Game. What distinction did he earn at Mount Tahoma High School?

a. The first athlete to ever go straight to the pros

b. The first baseball player to reach the majors

c. The first athlete to win nine varsity letters

d. The first individual to ever visit L.A.

13. After 11 solid years with the Dodgers, Ron was traded to Chicago. What did he provide the Cubs with during his four-year stint?

a. A barrel of laughs in the clubhouse

b. A speedy leadoff batter

c. The ability to coach, counsel, and play

d. Veteran leadership

14. Harry Arthur "Cookie" Lavagetto played third for Brooklyn in the 1940s. He's most famous for driving in the

winning run against the Yanks in Game 4 of the 1947 World Series. When he did that, what was New York pitcher Bill Bevens an out away from?

   a. The first complete game in Series history
   b. The first no-hitter in Series history
   c. The first perfect game in Series history
   d. The Yanks' first win ever against Brooklyn

15. Lavagetto also made the record books as a manager. For which team was he the last manager of in 1960 and for which was he the first in 1961?

   a. The Boston Braves & The Boston Red Sox
   b. The Chicago Cubs & The Chicago White Sox
   c. The Montreal Royals & The Kansas City Royals
   d. The Washington Senators & The Minnesota Twins

16. Cookie unfortunately missed four full seasons of baseball with Brooklyn from 1941 to 1945 due to the war. In which branch of the military did he serve?

   a. Air Force
   b. Army
   c. Navy
   d. Special Forces

17. Billy Cox covered the Brooklyn hot corner from 1948 to 1954 and played a decisive role in the 1953 Series. After he finished with Baltimore, how many other third basemen did the O's try in '55?

   a. 6

b. 8

c. 11

d. 13

18. Brooklyn's third baseman "Jersey Joe" Stripp was the last batter to try to hit a legally thrown spitter in 1934. Who was the Pirates pitcher to serve it up?

a. Barney Dreyfuss

b. Burleigh Grimes

c. Frankie Frisch

d. Preacher Roe

19. Joe Stripp broke in with the Reds in 1928, passed through Brooklyn, and hung up his cleats in 1938. Which team did he finish with?

a. The Boston Bees

b. The Cincinnati Reds

c. The St. Louis Cardinals

d. The Washington Nationals

20. Hanley Ramirez played several different positions, but opponents feared his bat. In the 2013 NLDS against the Braves, what franchise record did he equal?

a. He drew four intentional walks in one game.

b. He had four extra-base hits in one game but was picked off three times.

c. He went 8 for 16, with six extra-base hits.

d. He went 10 for 20, with eight extra-base hits.

QUIZ ANSWERS

1. C — "The best hitter God has made in a long time"

2. A — True

3. C — Rick Sutcliffe

4. B — Cleveland

5. A — Hit 100 homers for three different teams

6. B — Putouts

7. A — An icon in the city of L.A.

8. C — Kinesiology

9. D — Tim Wallach

10. C — $5.1 million

11. B — His college coach, Chuck "Bobo" Brayton (though some claim it was Lasorda!) /

12. C — The first athlete to ever win nine varsity letters

13. D — Veteran leadership

14. B — The first no-hitter in Series history

15. D — The Washington Senators / The Minnesota Twins

16. C — Navy

17. D — 13

18. B — Burleigh Grimes

19. A — The Boston Bees

20. C — He went 8 for 16, with six extra-base hits.

DID YOU KNOW?

1. Alas, Hanley had the habit of committing errors, despite his booming bat. He cost Clayton Kershaw a possible perfect game with a throwing error in the top of the seventh in June 2014.

2. Playing for seven teams during a 15-year stretch, Juan Uribe contributed to L.A. success in 2013 and 2014. He won the World Series twice, once with the rival Giants in 2010.

3. After graduating from the Dominican Summer League, Uribe found himself first with the Single-A Asheville Tourists and then the Salem Avalanche in the Carolina League.

4. The Dodgers Nation fan poll in 2020 showed Justin Turner edging Ron Cey, 36-35%, as the club's best-ever third baseman. Recency bias may be responsible.

5. One obvious reason for Justin's popularity is his soaring confidence: "My expectations for 2020 are the same as every year. To win every single game that we can, win the division, make it to the playoffs, and win a World Series."

6. After losing the 2017 World Series to the Astros, who have been tainted by a sign-stealing scandal, Turner took it a bit further. "They shouldn't have rings. Sorry. A world championship is earned," he said.

7. Turner and his wife joined Mookie Betts to speak out against the tragic death of George Floyd. The couple has regularly helped people in need in the Los Angeles community through the Justin Turner Foundation and the L.A. Dodgers Foundation (LADF).

8. Bill James had nothing bad to say about Guerrero: "Pedro was the best hitter in baseball in the 1980s, bar none, and very probably might have won the Triple Crown in '82, '83, or '85 had he not been playing in one of the toughest parks for a hitter."

9. Another Dodgers third baseman, Enos Cabell, ruminated: "Outfielders, and first basemen, too, they don't have to think. But the other infielders have to think."

10. Reporting in 1984, just after signing a five-year deal, Guerrero was "just a little late, and just a little overweight," according to Lasorda. Playing third, he had a tough time getting started. Tommy bailed him out by moving him to the outfield, and his average shot above .300.

CHAPTER 13:

WHO'S AT SHORT?

QUIZ TIME!

1. "The Little Colonel," Pee Wee Reese, manned shortstop like no other. How many times did the Dodgers win the NL pennant during his career in Brooklyn?

    a. 4 times in 18 years

    b. 5 times in 20 years

    c. 7 times in 16 years

    d. 9 times in 15 years

2. Which of the following statements is NOT true about Reese?

    a. He continues to be the Dodgers' all-time leader in runs scored.

    b. He remains the Dodgers' all-time leader in walks.

    c. He was a top-ten MVP finisher eight times.

    d. He was an average defender.

3. While Reese served in the Navy during WWII, the

Dodgers took a dive. How many games out of first were they in 1943 without him?

    a. 32

    b. 36

    c. 42

    d. 50

4. Pee Wee became a mentor to Robinson, though he admitted Jackie was the first African-American he'd ever shaken hands with. What did Reese's father show him to stress the horrors of racism?

    a. Buses passing with African-Americans forced to sit in the back

    b. Some films on racist crimes

    c. A tree where a lynching had happened

    d. A segregated hotel

5. Many fans put Maury Wills ahead of Pee Wee in the pantheon of Dodgers shortstops. Which of the following highlights are NOT true of Maury?

    a. Seven-time All-Star

    b. Two-time Gold Glove Winner

    c. Three-time World Series winner

    d. Hall-of-Famer

6. In Maury's MVP season, he stole 104 bases to break Ty Cobb's record, set in 1915. How many teams did he "out-steal" that season?

    a. 14

b. 18

c. 22

d. Every other team in baseball

7. Maurice "Sonny" Wills had a stellar high school career as an athlete. What was the 1948 Cardozo (Washington, D.C.) football team he led most famous for?

    a. They didn't lose a game for four consecutive years.

    b. They outscored opponents by an average of 46 points.

    c. They yielded zero points.

    d. They introduced formations that were never before seen.

8. In the 1962 season, in which he stole 104 bases, how many times was Maury caught in the act?

    a. 9

    b. 13

    c. 15

    d. 21

9. In an attempt to corral Wills, what did San Francisco Giants manager Alvin Dark order his grounds crew do?

    a. Drop numerous pieces of dark rock on the basepaths

    b. Mix abundant sand with dirt on the basepaths

    c. Set the bases loosely in their holes so they'd be harder to steal

    d. Water the base paths heavily so they turned to mud

10. Maury's base-stealing prowess was due not only to his speed. On one occasion, how many throws did he draw at first from the Mets' Roger Craig before stealing second?

a. 7

b. 10

c. 12

d. 15

11. Bill Russell bled blue: 18 years as a Los Angeles player and two more as manager. How many games did he play for the Dodgers?

    a. 1,722

    b. 1,884

    c. 2,075

    d. 2,181

12. No Dodgers player in the West Coast part of the team's history played more games than Russell, and only one played more as a Dodger. Who was he?

    a. Adrián Beltré

    b. Eddie Collins

    c. Mel Ott

    d. Zack Wheat

13. After managing the Albuquerque Dukes in the Pacific Coast League, Russell was brought back to the big leagues by GM Fred Claire. What accelerated Russell's promotion to acting Dodgers manager in 1996?

    a. Claire looked to shake up the team.

    b. The Dodgers were mired in a losing streak.

    c. Tommy Lasorda suffered a mild heart attack.

    d. Tommy Lasorda suffered from constant indigestion.

14. When the 1998 team got off to a bad start and the News Corporation was set to buy the franchise, Russell and Claire were ousted. What was the title of Claire's tell-all book?

    a. *Three Decades, and Nothing But Blue*
    b. *My 30 Years In La-La Baseball*
    c. *My 30 Years In Dodger Blue*
    d. *No Thanks After 30 Blue Years*

15. Rafael Furcal's father, Silvino, was an exceptional outfielder before Dominicans got much of a look from American scouts. How many of Rafael's brothers made it to professional baseball?

    a. 1
    b. 2
    c. 3
    d. 4

16. In 2003, while playing shortstop for the Braves, Furcal completed an unassisted triple play. It was only the eighth such play in MLB history.

    a. True
    b. False

17. In December 2005, Rafael signed a three-year free agent deal with the Dodgers for $39 million. How much was the first Braves' contract he signed in 1996?

    a. $2000
    b. $5000

c. $10,000

d. $20,000

18. When César Izturis debuted with Toronto in 2001, he joined a distinguished line of Venezuelan shortstops in MLB. Which of the following is NOT one of them?

a. Luis Aparício

b. Dave Concepción

c. Ozzie Guillén

d. José Reyes

19. Even though he was the first Dodgers shortstop to win a Gold Glove since Maury Wills, Izturis' bat was less than explosive. In June 2004, he was hitting .348. Where did his BA end up that year?

a. .230

b. .250

c. .265

d. .288

20. Alex Cora spent seven years with Los Angeles and had the fourth-longest at-bat in MLB history (since stat guys started keeping track in the 1980s) in 2004. How many consecutive pitches did he foul back before connecting for a homer?

a. 10

b. 12

c. 14

d. 17

QUIZ ANSWERS

1. C — 7 times in 16 years

2. D — He was a superb defender (not average).

3. B — 36

4. C — A tree where a lynching had happened

5. D — Hall-of-Famer

6. D — Every team in baseball

7. C — They yielded zero points.

8. B — 13

9. D — Water the base paths heavily so they turned to mud

10. C — 12

11. D — 2,181

12. D — Zack Wheat

13. C — Tommy Lasorda suffered a mild heart attack.

14. C — *My Thirty Years In Dodger Blue*

15. B — 2

16. B — False (it was the 12th)

17. B — $5000

18. D — José Reyes

19. D — .288

20. C — 14

DID YOU KNOW?

1. Alex Cora likes to stretch things out. He played in two of the longest nine-inning games in MLB history. The first was a Dodgers-Giants game in 2001 that lasted 4 hours and 27 minutes.

2. Manny Machado knows how to mix it up. He was fined by MLB for the reckless way he ran into first base against the Brewers in the 2018 NLCS. Unfortunately, Machado was the final Dodgers out as L.A. fell to Boston in the World Series.

3. José Vizcaíno, a utility infielder in the 1990s and 2000s, was one of only three players (the others are Daryl Strawberry and Ricky Ledée) who played in games with all four past and future New York teams: the Dodgers, Giants, Mets, and Yanks.

4. When Nomar Garciaparra returned home to Southern Cal to play for the Dodgers in 2006, he made a seamless move from short to first, making way for Furcal. He hit some timely homers as the season closed and was voted the NL's Comeback Player of The Year.

5. Nomar officially retired with the Red Sox in 2010 but returned to L.A. in 2014 to broadcast Dodgers' games on the radio with Rick Monday, and on TV with Orel Hershiser.

6. L.A. shortstop José Offerman made history as the first to ever bat against the expansion Marlins. Charlie Hough struck him out. José's temper got the better of him when he attacked an ump while coaching the Licey Tigers in the Dominican Winter League in 2010.

7. After that right hook aimed at umpire D.J. Reyburn, the American crew left the Dominican Republic, afraid for their safety. Offerman's suspension was finally lifted in 2013.

8. We return to Pee Wee Reese, the eminently quotable Dodger: "If I had my career to play over, one thing I'd do differently is swing more. Those 1,200 walks I got… nobody remembers them."

9. Reese was perhaps Jackie Robinson's biggest champion. To give Robinson's performance more perspective, Reese said, "I don't know any other ballplayer who could've done what he did. To be able to hit with everybody yelling at him. … To do what he did has got to be the most tremendous thing I've ever seen in sports."

10. How did Reese feel about his team? Don Newcombe said, "He loved the Dodgers, he always respected the Dodgers and the people who owned the Dodgers."

CHAPTER 14:

THE OUTFIELD GANG

QUIZ TIME!

1. Zack "Buck" Wheat still holds some Dodgers' hitting records. He and his brother were both with Brooklyn for five seasons. What was his brother's name?

   a. Carl "Cream" Wheat
   b. Davis "Darling" Wheat
   c. McKinley "Mack" Wheat
   d. William "Willie" Wheat

2. Zack was one of the first players to use the tactic of "holding out" to make more money from the team. What did he threaten to do during World War I rather than play?

   a. Ride horses in the rodeo
   b. Raise and sell horses to Missouri farmers
   c. Raise and sell pack mules to the U.S. Army
   d. Write a best-selling book about batting

3. Wheat was one of the only players to ever win a batting title (1918) without doing a certain thing. What did he and Rod Carew (1972) do?

    a. Never hit a homer
    b. Never hit a triple
    c. Never walked
    d. Never was hit by a pitch

4. Duke Snider ruled centerfield for Brooklyn in the 1950s. In his 16 seasons with the Dodgers, how many times did he lead his team to the World Series?

    a. 2
    b. 4
    c. 6
    d. 8

5. Snider was often compared to two other talented center fielders also playing in N.Y. Which of the following was NOT one of them?

    a. Baby Doll Jacobson
    b. Mickey Mantle
    c. Willie Mays

6. Carl Furillo's powerful arm earned him the nickname "the Reading Rifle." How did he get his other nickname, "Skoonj"?

    a. He used a rudimentary scooter in the clubhouse.
    b. His favorite Italian dish was "scungilli" (snails).
    c. His favorite Italian soup was called "sciusceddu."
    d. He dropped out of school in eighth grade.

7. Even though Furillo's Dodgers lost a legendary pennant race to the N.Y. Giants in 1951, Carl set a new team record with 667 at-bats. Whose 1921 mark did he break?

   a. Ivy Olson
   b. Hy Myers
   c. Ferdie Schupp
   d. Sweetbreads Bailey

8. Speed demon Willie Davis retired in 1979 with the sixth most triples of any major leaguer since 1945. How many did he hit?

   a. 108
   b. 120
   c. 138
   d. 156

9. After running a 9.5-second 100-yard dash and long jumping 25+ feet (7.75 meters) in high school, Davis did something unheard of in minor league ball in Reno. What did he pull off?

   a. He caught balls hit over both the left and right fielders' heads.
   b. He jumped over the catcher to score the winning run.
   c. He scored nine times from first on a single.
   d. He stole two bases on one throw.

10. In the 1978 L.A. season, ace pitcher Don Sutton publicly claimed that Reggie Smith was a more valuable Dodger than Steve Garvey. What was the result of his comment?

a. Garvey agreed and took a salary cut

b. Garvey demanded to be traded to San Francisco

c. Sutton's glove was mysteriously stolen

d. A wrestling match with Garvey in the clubhouse

11. After his playing career in the U.S. and Japan, Smith helped various American teams as a hitting coach. What medal did the U.S. Olympic baseball team bring home from Beijing in 2008?

a. Gold

b. Silver

c. Bronze

d. None

12. In 1974, Dusty Baker earned a spot in baseball history while with the Braves for doing nothing. What happened?

a. He was on deck when Chipper Jones hit for the cycle.

b. He was on deck when Hank Aaron hit his record-breaking 715th homer.

c. He gave Aaron his favorite bat when Hank bashed his 715th dinger.

d. He was on deck when Hank Aaron broke the MLB record for intentional walks.

13. Baker helped L.A. win three National League Championship Series, in 1977, 1978 and 1981. In the latter year, the Dodgers finally broke through to win it all. But what was Baker's anemic average in that Series?

a. .147

b. .154

c. .167

d. .182

14. Raúl Mondesi was a fleet L.A. outfielder in the 1990s. He also got into Dominican politics after he retired. What office did he hold?

a. President

b. Vice President

c. San Cristóbal Mayor

d. Senator

15. In 1997, Mondesi hit .310 while mashing 30 homers and stealing 32 bags. He was the first Dodger ever to join the "30-30 Club."

a. True

b. False

16. Smooth-swinging outfielder Shawn Green holds several MLB batting records. When he piled up 19 total bases in a game, whose record did he break (set versus Brooklyn, by the way)?

a. Joe Adcock of the Milwaukee Braves

b. Gair Allie of the Pittsburgh Pirates

c. Ernie Banks of the Chicago Cubs

d. Tex Clevenger of the Boston Red Sox

17. When he retired in 2007, Green was one of only four active players with 300 homers, 1,000 runs, 1,000 RBI, 150 stolen bases, 400 doubles and a .280 BA. Which of the following is NOT among them?

a. Barry Bonds

b. Ken Griffey, Jr.

c. Albert Pujols

d. Gary Sheffield

18. Speaking of right fielder Shef, what's Gary's current job?

a. English teacher

b. Hitting coach

c. Sports agent

d. Uber Eats manager

19. Sheffield's wicked swing attracted many admirers. His first manager quipped, "Gary can turn on a 38-caliber bullet." Who was this manager?

a. Glenn Hoffman

b. Manny Mota

c. Tom Trebelhorn

d. Bill Russell

20. When Matt Kemp manned centerfield for the Dodgers in 2011, he became the first player since Luis Aparício in 1963 to finish in the top two in homers and stolen bases.

a. True

b. False

QUIZ ANSWERS

1. C — McKinley "Mack" Wheat

2. C — Raise and sell pack mules to the U.S. Army

3. A — Never hit a homer

4. C — 6

5. A — Baby Doll Jacobson

6. B — His favorite Italian dish was "scungilli" (snails).

7. A — Ivy Olson

8. C — 138

9. C — He scored nine times from first on a single.

10. D — A wrestling match with Garvey in the clubhouse

11. C — Bronze

12. B — He was on deck when Hank Aaron hit his record-breaking 715th homer.

13. C — .167

14. C — San Cristóbal Mayor

15. A — True

16. A — Joe Adcock of the Milwaukee Braves

17. C — Albert Pujols

18. C — Sports agent

19. C — Tom Trebelhorn

20. B — False (since Hank Aaron in 1963)

DID YOU KNOW?

1. Despite Kemp's ability to crush the ball, he came under some criticism from general manager Ned Colletti for bad base running. He was caught stealing 15 times in 2010.

2. But Kemp had the last laugh, finishing the 2010 campaign with five home runs in his last five games. He joined the Dodgers elite of Roy Campanella, Adrián González, Joc Pederson and Shawn Green, who had all hit a home run in five straight games.

3. Just before the 2011 All-Star Game, Giants' manager Bruce Bochy announced he would bat Kemp third: "He's a guy with speed and power; a guy that can beat you with a base hit or the long ball. He's what you call a complete player."

4. When Kirk Gibson's monstrous pinch-hit homer cleared the Dodger Stadium fence in 1988, it was called "the greatest moment in L.A. sports history" in a poll. What's more, the Dodgers were considered underdogs throughout the playoffs, first against the Mets and then the A's.

5. Despite being the de facto L.A. leader, Gibson was never expected to play in the decisive game because of injuries to both legs. When TV cameras scanned the bench in the late innings, he was nowhere to be found. Luckily, Gibby was watching the game on the clubhouse TV and quickly told Lasorda he was ready to pinch hit.

6. Gibson later recounted that, before the Series, L.A. scout Mel Didier predicted that Dennis Eckersley would surely throw a backdoor slider on a 3-2 count to a lefty. That was the pitch and you know the rest.

7. Bashing the ball with the best of them, Manny Ramirez was crazy for baseball as a Dominican kid. At age 8, his grandmother got him a Dodgers' uniform (No. 30) which Manny said was one of his most prized possessions.

8. Suddenly Dodgers fans had "Mannywood" on their hands. Manny was named the NL Player of The Month in August 2008. After L.A. lost in the playoffs, Manny was asked about his future: "Gas is up. And so am I," he reasoned.

9. Yasiel Puig, the Cuban-born outfielder, was nicknamed "the Wild Horse" by long-time announcer Vin Scully. Puig is the Dodgers' leader in all-time playoff appearances with 58.

10. Starting in 2013, Puig tried to defect from Cuba 13 times to become a legal resident of Mexico and then sign an MLB deal. He was ably assisted by Floridian Raul Pacheco, who had once tried to buy $150 worth of beer with a fake credit card.

CHAPTER 15:

THE HEATED RIVALRIES

QUIZ TIME!

1. Baseball fans know that two rivalries are more heated than any others. What are they?

    a. Mets vs. Yankees & Dodgers vs. Angels

    b. Red Sox vs. Yankees & Dodgers vs. Giants

    c. Cubs vs. White Sox & Indians vs. Reds

    d. Braves vs. Phillies & Brewers vs. Tigers

2. The first great rivals of the Dodgers played in the same city, New York. How many times have the Dodgers and Yankees faced off in the Series in the past 80 years?

    a. 13

    b. 11

    c. 9

    d. 7

3. Who has the upper hand in this rivalry?

    a. Yankees, 8 wins to 3

    b. Yankees, 6 wins to 5

c. Dodgers, 7 wins to 4

d. Dodgers, 10 wins to 1

4. When Brooklyn first played at its new home, Ebbets Field, it hosted the New York Highlanders (later to become the Yanks) in a 1913 exhibition. Who had the winning Dodgers hit?

   a. Jake Daubert

   b. Casey Stengel

   c. Bull Wagner

   d. Mysterious Walker

5. When did the rivalry between the Bronx Bombers (also the Yanks) and "Dem Bums" from Brooklyn really get going?

   a. The 1913 exhibition

   b. In a 1938 newspaper article

   c. The 1941 Series

   d. The 1947 Series

6. After the 1957 season, Walter O'Malley decided to move his Dodgers team west and he persuaded his archrivals, the Giants, to do the same. Who was the Giants' owner at the time?

   a. George Christopher

   b. Chub Feeney

   c. Joan Whitney Payson

   d. Horace Stoneham

7. Los Angeles and San Francisco have long been competitors in the economic, cultural and political arenas.

Thus, the teams' new California homes were fertile ground for the rivalry's transplantation.

   a. True
   b. False

8. Since moving to California, which team holds the edge in NL pennants (11-6) and World Series wins (5-3)?

   a. Los Angeles
   b. San Francisco

9. 69. In 2019, L.A. and San Francisco played each other for the 2,500th time. Do you think it ever gets old? Which of the following sets of teams has NOT played the same number of games?

   a. Chicago Cubs vs. Pittsburgh Pirates
   b. Pittsburgh Pirates vs. St. Louis Cardinals
   c. Boston Red Sox vs. N.Y. Yankees

10. Two particular late-season comebacks by the Dodgers to overtake the rival Giants in the NL West stand out. How many games behind was L.A. in 2014?

   a. 6.5
   b. 9.5
   c. 11
   d. 13.5

11. That same year, the Dodgers' Clayton Kershaw shut down the Giants, 9-1, to secure another NL West Crown. Which other hurler combined with Clayton to go 8-0 against San Francisco that season?

a. Josh Beckett

b. Zack Greinke

c. Brandon League

d. Brian Wilson

12. In 1997, a late two-game sweep by the Giants in Candlestick Park sent L.A. packing from the playoffs. Who said, "It led to an organizational upheaval … (from which i)t's taken the Dodgers nearly a decade to recover"?

a. *L.A. Times* sportswriter Bill Murray

b. Manager Bill Russell

c. L.A. GM Fred Claire

d. *L.A. Times* sportswriter Bill Plaschke

13. During the final Dodger-Giant series in San Francisco in 1991, the home team drew 150,000 fans. What percent of their total fan number from 81 home games was that?

a. 5%

b. 10%

c. 15%

d. 20%

14. Which famous Dodgers star chose to retire in 1956 rather than report to the dreaded rival Giants?

a. Carl Erskine

b. Jackie Robinson

c. Johnny Podres

d. Dixie Howell

15. Conversely, which Giants star preferred to be traded to the Mets in 1972 rather than suit up in Dodger blue?

a. Gaylord Perry
b. Tito Fuentes
c. Willie McCovey
d. Willie Mays

16. What happened in 2014 to intensify the Dodger-Giant rivalry?

   a. Yasiel Puig flipped his bat after homering off Madison Bumgarner.
   b. Madison Bumgarner beaned Yasiel Puig.
   c. Yasiel Puig flipped off the Giants' fans.
   d. Madison Bumgarner showed his middle digit to the L.A. faithful.

17. Another rival, the Angels, became a thorn in the Dodgers' side because of geographic proximity. When did that rivalry kick off?

   a. 1958
   b. 1961
   c. 1965
   d. 1972

18. In 2005, the Angels' owner pulled a fast one on Anaheim by naming his team "Los Angeles." Who was this owner?

   a. Arturo Moreno
   b. Gene Autry
   c. Tony Tavares
   d. Bill Stoneman

19. Over the past five years, the Dodgers-Angels rivalry has taken on more of a personal nature with the one of the

game's best pitcher hurling against arguably the best position player. Who are these guys?

a. Julio Urias & Albert Pujols
b. Kenta Maeda & Kole Calhoun
c. Clayton Kershaw & Mike Trout
d. Scott Kazmir & Tim Lincecum

20. The Chicago Cubs have turned into a tough Dodgers opponent of late. Which of the following players was NOT snatched away from L.A. by the Cubbies?

a. Yu Darvish
b. Brandon Morrow
c. Drew Smyly

QUIZ ANSWERS

1. B — Red Sox vs. Yankees & Dodgers vs. Giants

2. B — 11

3. A — Yankees, 8 wins to 3

4. B — Casey Stengel

5. C — The 1941 Series

6. D — Horace Stoneham

7. A — True

8. A — Los Angeles

9. C — Boston Red Sox vs. N.Y. Yankees

10. B — 9.5

11. B — Zack Greinke

12. D — L.A. Times sportswriter Bill Plaschke

13. B — 10%

14. B — Jackie Robinson

15. D — Willie Mays

16. A — Yasiel Puig flipped his bat after homering off Madison Bumgarner.

17. B — 1961

18. A — Arturo Moreno

19. C — Clayton Kershaw & Mike Trout

20. C — Drew Smyly

DID YOU KNOW?

1. In May of 1957, NL owners voted to allow the Dodgers and Giants franchises to leave New York and move west. The deal was contingent on both clubs moving together.

2. Players from the teams have developed their own individual rivalries. On April 16, 2004, Cy Young Award winner Eric Gagné of the Dodgers brought heat but Barry Bonds battled and then blasted one out. "I'm not sure which guy is from the other planet, but that was incredible," gushed S.F. commentator Mike Krukow.

3. Even though Juan Marichal bopped Dodgers catcher John Roseboro in the head with a bat, requiring 14 stitches, they eventually made up. "Hey, over the years, you learn to forget things," Roseboro reasoned.

4. In 1982, the Dodgers faced the Giants at San Francisco's Candlestick Park, needing a win to tie the Braves. But 39-year-old Joe Morgan had other ideas and corked one out. S.F. eliminated L.A., the next best thing to going to the playoffs themselves.

5. Eleven years later, the Dodgers were the spoilers. S.F. needed one win on the last day of the season to match the Braves. L.A. cruised, 12-1. Take that.

6. On October 2, 2004, L.A. needed a win to clinch the NL West. The Dodgers' 39-year-old outfielder Steve Finley

was the star, hitting a grand slam home run in the bottom of the 9th inning for a 7-3 victory. "I was dreaming about it, and it happened," Finley fondly recalled.

7. Darryl Strawberry will never be the most popular guy in La-La Land after he said, "Playing in L.A. was a huge letdown after a decade in N.Y. … In Dodger Stadium, the fans were much more, you know, Californian."

8. If one person could put the L.A.-S.F. rivalry on the back burner, it had to be Tommy Lasorda. In fact, he took the Giants out of the equation completely: "If you don't cheer for the Dodgers, there's a good chance you may not get into Heaven."

9. Maybe it all started in 1900. The Dodgers won the pennant and the Giants finished last. But Giants owner Andrew Freedman asked the NL to split the profits equally, regardless of how the teams finished.

10. When Charles Ebbets (the namesake of Brooklyn's field) died on April 18, 1925, the game went ahead as scheduled. Dodgers manager Wilbert Robinson explained, "Charlie wouldn't want anybody to miss a Giant-Brooklyn series just because he died."

CONCLUSION

The great Dodgers names roll off your tongue: Reese, Robinson, Leo "The Lip" Durocher, Lasorda, Don, Sandy, and Cey, even O'Malley, the man who moved the mighty franchise west of the Mississippi to the golden state of California where lay financial riches and hardcore baseball fans galore.

And here you have it: an amazing collection of Dodgers trivia, information and statistics at your fingertips! Regardless of how you fared on the quizzes, we hope you found this book entertaining, enlightening and educational.

Ideally, you knew many of these details already but also learned a good deal more about the history of the Dodgers, both in Brooklyn and L.A., their players, coaches, managers, and some of the quirky stories surrounding the team, its history and its special stadium. If you got a little peek into the colorful details that make being a fan so much more enjoyable, then our mission was accomplished!

The good news is the trivia doesn't have to stop there. Spread the word. Challenge your fellow Dodgers fans to see if they can do any better. Share some of the stories with the next generation to help them become Dodgers supporters, too.

If you are a big enough L.A. fan, consider creating your own quiz with some of the details that you know weren't presented here. Then test your friends to see if they can match your knowledge.

The Dodgers are one of baseball's most storied franchises. They have a long history with many stretches of success, and a few that were a bit less than successful. They've had glorious superstars, iconic moments and hilarious tales ... but most of all, they have wonderful, passionate fans. Thank you for being one of them. "A Whole New Blue."